Connor is ten years old, and lives in the North West of England with Mum, Dad, big brother Tom, and Toffee the dog. He was diagnosed with autism at the age of three. Just to add more chaos, baby brother Daniel appeared in his world in early October 2010. He has learned to cope well with this change, and as they say, life goes on....

# Outside

# In

By

Amanda Christine

Henaghan

Published by Amanda Christine Henaghan

Copyright © Amanda Christine Henaghan 2012

ISBN 978-0-9573866-0-0

For Frank and the boys

with love xxx


and for Jayne & Guy, far away in distance,

but always close to heart xxx

# CONTENTS

# FOREWORD

By Amanda Henaghan

I initially set out to write this book to answer the many questions I have been asked about Connor over the years. Parents of other children would ask things such as "how old was he when you found out?" and "what were the first signs or symptoms?" I wondered if some were secretly observing their own child's behaviour, hoping to lay to rest their own fears, but I dutifully answered as honestly as I could, happy that they were interested at all. Some replies were easy to recall, others required a little more thought, or a longer explanation. Ten minutes later, when I was still rambling on, the person opposite smiling politely, willing me to shut up, I realised that they really didn't want so much detail, but it was hard to stop when I got going. I loved to talk about Connor, as much as it upset me to dwell on his difficulties, it was akin to a therapy session, and felt good for the soul.

At first I convinced myself I could never find enough material to produce a decent thickness book. I decided from the beginning that I wouldn't be happy with some flimsy wafer thin attempt, it had to be a proper sized effort or nothing, there was to be no compromise. As I started to write and plan the chapters, the words began to flow freely, but I soon realised that as much as the work was supposed to be about autism, I was really describing the effects it had on all our lives, not just what it meant for Connor himself. I was studying the emotional side of things, the psychology of the mind, delving deep into my own thoughts and insecurities. It has been a tough journey, and has made me analyse the actions, responses and decisions I have made over the years. It has made me question myself, and wonder if I could have done some things better, but what's done is done. You can't rewind the past. It has been upsetting having to relive some of my worst years, but the story had to be complete, true, and honest. A full account of all the ups and downs, the tears and laughter, the smiles and the tantrums. I hope you find this book entertaining, informative and moving. But more importantly, that my words give strength to those who need it.

# A THOUGHT FROM CONNOR...

What do you see when you look at me? Who do you think I am? Even before you opened the cover, even before you read one word, did you make any assumptions about my life? Did you wonder what I like to do, what I like to eat, to wear, to play? Did you see a typical white, British, ten year old who goes to the local school, has lots of friends, can read and write and fit in? Did you see a child who sits calmly at the dinner table, and knows how to be polite and sociable? A child who leads a normal family life?

If you assumed any of these things you'd be far from right, but none of that should matter anyway. It shouldn't matter if I'm white, black, pink, green, brown, or purple. It shouldn't matter what language I speak, what country I come from, what religion I am. I shouldn't be judged according to my colour, culture, faith, gender, beliefs, appearance, or disability. In fact, I shouldn't be judged at all.

When you study my face do you see the severe learning and communication disability that is hidden inside, a disability that makes me anxious, confused, frustrated? A disability so bad that it takes over my whole life, controls everything I do, and shapes my world? No, I'm sure you don't, as I look just like any other child you might meet, and that's just how I want to be treated, as normal. No better, no worse, just equal.

Every day I face discrimination. Every day I face segregation. Every day I face intolerance. THIS HAS TO STOP, NOW. I am still only ten years old; I have a long way to go yet. I want to grow up in a world where I can feel safe, loved, and included. Not ridiculed, despised, and rejected. A world where I can shout hello out the car window to children in the street, and they actually shout hello back, instead of just staring at me. A world where I can have my own friends and sleepover at other peoples' houses. A world where I feel wanted, and not so alone. I can't change the way society views people with problems such as mine, but you can. So do it for me, and all those like me, please.

# PART 1

## THE PRESENT…

It is summer. Sitting here on the balcony in Spain, with the sun blazing down from a cloudless sky, glass of wine in one hand; swimming pool beckons enticingly only yards away. With a wonderful view of the calm blue sea beyond, I shouldn't have a care in the world. I can hear the distant chatter and laughter of other families as they play happily in the pools of neighbouring villas. Suddenly, my young son potters out to break the silence. Muttering to himself, repeating things he has heard on one of his countless collection of DVD's, he gently brushes a hand across my shoulder as he wanders past and down to the pool, makes one circuit of the edge, then disappears back inside. Keeping half an ear open, I don't even bother to look round, knowing from experience that he has such excellent balance and co-ordination, unlike his mother, that even when he runs at full speed around the water's edge he is very unlikely to fall in. If I panicked every time he attempted anything remotely dangerous I would be in an asylum by now as this is not your ordinary, average child. This is a child who has spent the whole of his life thriving on being unconventional. A child who can be completely reckless, not caring what the world, or anyone in it, thinks or cares about his outrageous and unorthodox behaviour. This is a child with autism.

It has taken me a very long time to be able to talk rationally and calmly about the subject. That is not to say that I am now any less passionate or emotional about Connor, I am just more in control of my feelings these days. Whenever I watch programmes about autism I choose to watch them alone. I still prefer to keep my tears, grief and fears about the future to myself. A very good friend gave me a video; it was the TV adaptation of the book 'A Friend like Henry'. This is a book about a severely autistic boy called Dale and the wonderful dog who helped to bring him back into our world. We had missed it when it was first shown around Christmas a few years ago. She handed it over reluctantly, after repeated requests by me, saying that I really shouldn't watch it, that her and her husband had found it terribly distressing. I retorted that how shocking could it be, I lived and breathed autism every second, minute and hour, every single day, what could possibly upset me now? She was right to be hesitant, of course. From the opening sequence where Dale is screaming in the shoe shop, one I can relate to in explicit detail, I bawled my eyes out, until the very last credit rolled up the screen. Yes, I could have turned it off mid flow at any time, could have dried my tears and walked away, but I just had to make it to the end however upsetting it became. I have since read the book; the real story told by the young boys' mum, it is an amazingly honest, inspirational and compelling account of their life.

I have now read many books on autism, some written by families affected by the condition, some written by experts and professionals working in the field. The ones I enjoyed the most are those written by the families themselves. They are the ones who know the real story; they are the ones who write straight from the heart. Anyone could read a hundred books, watch countless documentaries and films, but unless you actually live or work closely with someone who has this condition, it is extremely difficult to really understand. I never feel offended when asked questions about him, however insane the question, I still prefer people to ask rather than ignore him, change the subject, or pretend not to have noticed his often bizarre behaviour. It is very demoralising to be tutted at, whispered about or totally ignored during a rather loud tantrum in the middle of a busy supermarket.

On a good day, not that there have been too many of those in the past, Connor looks just like any other child. He has no physical deformities, no outward signs that he is any different from the next person. That makes him a bit harder to explain when the differences in his behaviour become obvious to all around him. Maybe most people view him as a disruptive little sod who needs a good telling off and a slap on the backside and what is his mother doing by letting him get away with it? You can see the looks on people's faces and read the thoughts in their minds – 'useless parents, probably spend all their time at work, leaving the kids with childminders and babysitters, more interested in their laptops and busy lives to care what their children get up to, won't even know what their favourite food is or bother to ask what they did at school that day'.

If you take a step back you can at least begin to understand some people's reactions, even if you don't see things their way or agree with their point of view. Before Connor came into my life I had no idea, no clue whatsoever, what autism really was and what it meant to the person and the families living with them. I was totally oblivious to this parallel world of social workers, special needs schools, speech therapists, child physcologists,

4

picture exchange systems and sign language. Had never heard of a statement of educational needs, disability living allowance or direct payments for respite care. I was probably one of those people, who would have glanced and looked away, being very sympathetic but not wishing to get involved. Probably one of those people who when quizzed by my other son, who is a little older than Connor, as to what was wrong with that person, at the top of his voice as young children find it impossible to whisper, would have quickly hushed him. Explaining that there was something different about that person and that it was rude to point or stare. We would have walked away without comment, with lots of compassion, but absolutely no understanding whatsoever of how they live their lives each and every day.

I would never condemn anyone for a misunderstanding of my son but it is nice when someone comes up to us and shows concern when we brave a trip out and it ends up in a standoff. Screaming fits on the floors of shops are expected. If we go out and don't experience a major incident I class this as a miracle. I rush through the door and yell excitedly to my husband that we actually managed a trip to Tesco's without me losing him in the aisles, or him running off and nearly causing a full on collision in the car park. I am still surprised and somewhat relieved when an hour out alone with Connor has not turned me into a quivering, agitated, frustrated wreck.

As time passes I think I am either getting better at coping or becoming more immune to his behaviour. Either way, there are still certain things that are acceptable in life and some things that just aren't. Sadly he is going to have to learn to live in our world and do things our way, whether he likes it or not.

This summer has been a revelation. It is the first summer with Connor I would actually class as a real holiday and not the usual nightmare from hell or a test of strength and endurance that we have been subjected to in the past. From what I have read many autistic children do not cope well with changes in routine or circumstances. We decided to build our home in Spain some years ago to give him, and us all, a sanctuary to escape to each summer. Regardless of the financial aspect of it all, we finally have a place he can call home. He accepts now that this is where he comes when we go to the airport and board a plane. He no longer feels the compulsion to explore every room, cupboard and wardrobe each time we come here. He knows where everything is, and is comfortable and familiar with his surroundings.

The boys are playing in the pool right now, laughing and jumping in happily. It won't last long but that is only to be expected. All children will fight, compete and challenge each other. That's just a way of life, a lesson in growing up, and very, very normal. Tom, who is 20 months older than Connor, is a typical little boy just trying to fit in and grow up. He has lots of school friends and is polite, friendly and sociable. To me he is an absolute saint. He puts up with life with his brother, which is often very different to the lives of his school friends who all have brothers and sisters without problems. The last ten years have been a learning curve for us all. There are many things we won't do with Connor right now, many places you just don't go to. You could, if you were willing to put up with the trials and tribulations that go with, but sometimes it isn't worth the stress.

Recently I have reattempted some outings, which in the past have been unbelievably intolerable. Things appear on the face of it to be slowly getting ever so slightly easier. Whether it is because he is getting older, learning more, or simply becoming more tolerant we just don't know. I feel that as long as we move forwards and not backwards then we have a fighting chance of gaining some normality of a life in the future.

It is scary that there seems to be many more children being born with some form of autism these days. I don't remember ever hearing about it when I was at school, or that any one of my peers had any noticeable learning difficulties. There could be a whole host of causes, or simply only one, and who knows when or if they will ever be found. But right now we have Connor and regardless of his problems he is a very loving, energetic, and sensitive little boy, who so desperately needs his parents to be strong and show him the way.

More and more books are appearing on our supermarket shelves, true stories written by the parents of children like Connor, needing to share their experiences with others. Never make the mistake in thinking that they will all be the same. There may be a common thread running through them all, but each child will be completely different in so many ways. Each family has their own unique story to tell. This is our story.

I love writing poetry, so I thought what better way to explain some of Connors' passions, dislikes and behaviours. If he could express his thoughts by himself, I think this is what he might say:

Don't go ballistic,
Cos I am autistic,
Don't stand and stare at my hair.
Cos I hate them you see,
Just between you and me,
Those hairdressers really do scare!

I can't stand the taste,
Of that horrid toothpaste,
It just makes my hair stand on end.
But Mummy is mean,
She wants them to be clean,
It really drives me round the bend.

The world is confusing,
Not always amusing,
I sometimes lock myself away.
I struggle to read faces,
And visit new places,
Maybe I'll like them someday.

My shoes are a pest,
I've no time to get dressed,
It's cold but I like to be bare.
I won't eat my tea,
I just watch the TV,
And bounce up and down in the air.

If I brush past your arm,
Please don't shout, just be calm,
I don't see this as a sin.
I'm not being rude,
Or cheeky or crude,
I just like the feel of your skin.

I can be naughty when out,
I can scream and I shout,
Sometimes I lie on the floor.
But I'm better than I was,
I think it's just because,
I'm big now and understand more.

I like to climb trees,
Join the birds and the bees,
The taller the better is great.
I can scale a high wall,
Nothing scares me at all,
Except maybe queues, I can't wait.

I love to run free,
On the beach, in the sea,
And feel the cold wind in my hair.
My Mummy will worry,
That I'm in such a hurry,
You know what, I really don't care!

So don't judge my family,
They do try their best,
To cope with me when I am bad.
They pay a high price,
But I'm really quite nice,
If you got to know me, you'd be glad.

# PART 2– THE PAST...

# 1

## A STAR IS BORN

The earliest memory I have of Connor is watching him as he lay quietly sleeping on my hospital bed the morning after his birth. He looked so contented and calm, not a care in the world. He was dressed in a lovely pale blue outfit complete with matching hat, ready to make the journey home for the very first time.

I had had a reasonably normal delivery. Had gone for a check up, only to be told that my labour was already well on its way. I hadn't actually noticed and was told, quite matter-of-factly, that as I was there then I may as well stay and they would get things moving. I was slightly nervous, as I hadn't been expecting this but agreed anyway. Frank went home to make arrangements for Tom to be looked after, and I changed into my extremely flattering hospital gown. My waters hadn't broken yet so they decided to speed up the proceedings by performing this task manually. After some rather long, and quite uncomfortable, botched attempts by the student doctors, they admitted defeat and called in someone more senior. That over with I lay back, happily assuming that the contractions would now slowly start to kick in. I was hoping that Frank would appear back soon; I was quickly going to get bored without something to do for the next few hours. How wrong I was. The pain intensified at an alarming rate, and by the time Frank got back I was more than ready to admit defeat and call for help. Once up and running, the epidural worked excellently down the left hand side of my body, leaving the other half free to experience the joys of very powerful labour pains for the next five hours. I'm sure that men don't really believe us when we moan about this form of medication not always working wholly effectively.

Exactly seven hours from arriving at the hospital, Connor made his appearance into the world. Yes he was a bit slimy, bloody, and had matted hair but he was beautiful, and he was mine. After a bit of a clean up, I was really past caring about looks like at this point, all dignity having been lost many hours before, we were put in a wheelchair and taken to the ward. Very grateful that we had paid for a single room, some privacy at last, I was helped into bed and left in peace. I then endured a dreadful night's sleep, or rather lack of it, as only hospital beds can ensure. After three hours lying awake, desperate for the loo, with the threat of a cold metal bedpan, I chose to ignore the strict instructions not to venture out of bed on my own and dragged my one still dead leg the few yards to the bathroom. Even after having had more than my fair share of hospital stays for various reasons in the past, I have yet to conquer my bedpan phobia. Metal or not, it just doesn't seem right to 'go' whilst still in your bed, it's really not natural.

With the relief of an empty bladder, I recall eventually falling into a deep sleep around 5am, only to be hauled awake about an hour later with the promise of an overly stewed, luke warm cup of tea, which somehow passes as acceptable for patients in this country. I have had the pleasure of residing in at least four different hospitals over the last twenty years and the tea situation doesn't seem to have improved much at all. After managing to swallow it anyway, you are that hot and parched you would drink almost anything; I lay there half awake for the next few hours. Unable to get back to sleep, but not able to muster the energy to surface, I was acutely aware of all the activity going on in the corridor

14

outside. By 8am the nurses arrive to do their daily check- ups, and the doctors do their rounds before the days operating lists begin. Once I was cleared to go home I made a pathetic attempt at a wash, ashamedly having to make use of the shower stool, still being rather tender in certain regions, and a little unsteady. I seem to remember that Connor was very quiet that first night. Assuming it was due to the trauma of being shoved forcibly down a decidedly tight tunnel into what must seem like a tremendously bright and scary place, I couldn't blame him. Anyway, whatever the reason, I was grateful for the peace. Little did I know that would be one of very few quiet nights to come for a very, very long time.

Once I had managed to hobble round the room and dress myself, an unusually difficult procedure in my current circumstances, one we normally take so much for granted, I could turn my attentions to my new baby. I was well trained for this by now, having had our son Tom only twenty months earlier. I had changed nappies before Tom came along, but will never forget the horror of newborns' first offerings. I had done my research, read all the books, and taken advice. Only use luke warm water and cotton wool at first, no baby wipes as they can irritate delicate young skin. Totally acceptable suggestion. They don't appear to put in the baby books helpful tips on removing thick, smelly black tar, super glued all over your baby's bottom and up his back. Maybe whilst visiting Mothercare, a quick stop off at your local hardware store would be in order, a few wallpaper scrapers and a chisel might come in handy. Obviously they would have to be plastic with rounded edges to satisfy the health and safety fanatics out there. Neither do they include that advice on the very helpful list of items to take to the maternity unit. Cotton balls? – check. Tissues? – check. Blowtorch? – maybe not.

After a very unsuccessful, middle of the night, pitiful attempt to clean Tom after a twenty-four hour labour, a rather annoyed looking midwife appeared and took over. Tutting loudly, clearly unhappy at being dragged away from her tea and toast, she shoved me out of the way. She had obviously stumbled across a very inexperienced and incompetent new mother, and was so not impressed. Really not giving a toss at this stage, I left her to it, crawled back to bed and drifted off to sleep. Well the kind of sleep you get on a ward of eight new mothers with screaming babies. All who manage to wake at annoyingly small intervals, just giving you enough time to start dropping off, but not enough time to be so deeply asleep that you stood a chance of not hearing them. You would swear they are programmed to do this the second they are born, all synchronised together to mark the start of things to come for unsuspecting new parents.

So having already coped with a baby for nearly two years, even though I had hoped for a tad more of a gap, I was okay. I felt reasonably equipped, confident, and ready to face those sleepless nights and exhausting days all over again. I was determined to learn from my past mistakes and would not be so fussy this time round. I remember taking Tom to the nurse at our local practice, worried at the dryness and red sore patches on his skin. I was convinced he had some sort of skin disorder, food allergy, or terrible disease. The nurse just smiled knowingly and suggested I stopped bathing him so much; I was literally washing him away. I took him home, missed out a bath or two and he was fine. I had also learnt that they could survive without having everything bleached and boiled. Could wear a soiled bib for the whole of a feed. Didn't catch some hideous infection if they picked their dummy up off the floor, or ate the contents of their nose once in a while. Still lived if they had to wait while their bottle warmed up, or cried themselves to sleep. I had gone through all that, was still standing, and was more than ready for the next one.

So there he was, baby Connor, just over twelve hours old. He was clean, calm and happily asleep, lying on my hospital bed, dressed and ready to face the world. I remember staring down at him as vividly as if it were yesterday. I recall how beautiful he looked, how his skin was clear and olive coloured, not pale with red blotches, as Toms' had been. He looked so contented and serene, sleeping so peacefully, warm and cosy in his all in one outfit. I remember feeling so in awe of the tiny perfect creature we had created, so grateful for those moments alone with him that morning to reflect on the wonder of life itself. I felt so honoured that I had been fortunate enough to have this little person enter my life. The world seemed to stop that very second. Nothing else mattered. I was completely and utterly oblivious to everything going on outside that room. All I had to focus on at that moment in time was Connor, and I fell in love with him that instant. Little did I know what I had let myself in for. That that love would be tested to the very limits it could possibly stretch to.

Years later I was reminded of this image, not that it has ever been very far from my mind. Having been invited to a parents' social evening at

Connors' special needs school, I dragged my Mum along for company and moral support. They had made a big effort to encourage people to go. Drinks and snacks were on offer, and even a child-care service so you could have five minutes peace. Connors' teacher, who was also the computer expert, had put together a compilation of photos using PowerPoint, showing the children as babies, at various stages in between, then as they look now. The still images slowly faded in and out, with calming classical music playing in the background. A lump formed at the back of my throat and I was ever so grateful for the dimming of the lights as the faces appeared on the large screen. Being a big fan of Connor, his teacher had put many of the pictures I had sent of him in the show. There he was as a cute little baby; pictures of him in the classroom and out on school trips filled the screen, and then my all time favourite. Taken of him in our house in Spain, leaning his face on his hands and staring straight ahead, right into the camera, with tanned little arms and sun bleached hair. He looked totally fed up having to wait a whole ten minutes while his beloved fairy cakes cooked in the oven.

My eyes filled and I blinked hard, desperate for the tears to dry up before they could be released and fall down my face. The one thing that really hit me that night was how normal the children looked as babies and when they were very young. How you could be deceived into believing that there was absolutely nothing amiss. The photos gave no clue as to the life that lay ahead for them and their families. There was no reason to think that they would lead anything other than a usual, typical existence. In a way it seemed kind of sad, like some cruel twist of fate. That behind these seemingly carefree, beautiful baby faces lay a deep, dark secret. Hiding the numerous physical, learning, and communication problems that lurked within. It was heartbreaking to see all the pictures of Connor over the years, and to think back to the time when we were still blissfully unaware of what was to unfold.

But the most important thing to remember is that whatever they look like, however they behave, however different or difficult they appear to be, they are still as lovely, innocent and pure as the day they were born. They are as much a part of our society as everyone else. Have as much right to live in this world and experience all the things life has to offer. Have the right to be educated to the best of their abilities and the right to be loved, protected and safe.

\* \* \*

That very first morning as I stared down at Connor I remember wondering what the future might hold for him. I envisaged him and his brother growing up, enjoying the journey of life, together every step of the way. I could see them becoming the best of friends. Sure they would fight and argue at times, most siblings do, but a little healthy competition is not necessarily a bad thing. I had loved having a brother who was similar in age to grow up with. We did tons of things together and are still very close now. I had visions of the boys doing all the things I did with my own brother. I recall playing cricket and tennis in our back garden during long hot summer holidays. Constantly having to take turns in climbing over the fence, battling with prickly rose bushes, to retrieve lost balls. Whenever Wimbledon time came around we would rush to the park to play on a real tennis court. We were never really any good, but it never really mattered. I remember long days out at the zoo, and searching in rock pools on warm beaches in Wales. Designing homemade Mothers' Day cards, listening to the same music, going to the same school, hanging out with the same friends. When we were older we went to rock concerts together. We would go to pubs and clubs and walk the five miles home at three in the morning. Me being barefoot and in agony as my shoes were killing me, but sufficiently drunk enough for it not to register until the next morning. I remember all the summer holidays at my Aunties house in the Lake District. For anyone unfamiliar with our weather systems in the UK it often rains there pretty much any time of the year. It never seemed to matter to us though, as it is one of the most beautiful places you could ever visit. I lost count of all the picnics we had sat in the car, daring to open the steamed up windows just enough to clear them whilst trying not to let in the teeming rain. I recollect all the fishing expeditions, sitting for hours under oversized green umbrellas around the edges of large lakes. We were happy to sit there all day, often catching nothing but a nasty chill, ecstatic if you had so much as a nibble from an inch long fish on a very sorry looking stiff maggot. I could never quite bring myself to touch these vile creatures, or the fish for that matter, having to rely on my brother for all that. We would hike for hours up mountains and over hills, paddling happily in clear streams and rivers. We went fishing in the sea from the beaches, or balancing precariously on slippery rocks. Fresh mackerel for breakfast is a must, despite having to dissect all those tiny bones, well worth the risk of a sprain or two.

With age, mileage and the excesses of life, I sometimes have to stop and think what I did yesterday, but I can always recall many happy moments of my childhood, especially our summer holidays. We never went very far, could never afford the luxury of the foreign holidays that most people go on these days. The main destinations for us were North Wales and the Lake District, same old places, year in year out, and we loved every minute of it. We did however venture down south one summer to the Cornish coast. We stayed in a farmhouse in the middle of a seemingly very scary and desolate moor. I am sure that we were not really that far from civilisation but to me aged eleven, it appeared that way. The farmer and his wife felt they had a mission to force feed my brother a lovely fresh glass of goat's milk every evening before bed. He, on the other hand, thought it was vile, so my dad had to sneak up and drink it for him so as not to offend our hosts. Once we went out for a late night stroll. It was probably not too late, but to me being out on a cold, dark, bleak, vast expanse of open land was utterly terrifying. Rabbits flew in every direction, their eyes momentarily caught in the torchlight. Frozen for a split second then gone, hidden once more in the safety of the darkness. Spotting a group of wild horses in the distance, we turned off the torches so as to not attract any unwanted attention. Now I was really scared. I knew that we would not stand a chance if they decided to chase us; we had no way of outrunning them, and nowhere to hide. We crouched down in the long grass to watch, totally in awe of their raw beauty. They appeared purely white to me, only illuminated by the moonlight itself. It was so amazing to be able to experience these wonderful creatures running free like nature intended. After a while we quietly backtracked our way to the farm, that memory to remain with us forever.

There was always one recurring problem I had during our holidays though, that was my dilemma with using public toilets. I still struggle to use them even now, but when I was younger I was fanatical. Whether it is something to do with my heightened sense of smell, I just don't know. I was always ridiculed on school trips to the zoo, where I had to sit outside the giraffe house while everyone else went inside. Just one mere whiff of the place was enough to make me gag. A happy afternoon stroll through a field of cows was to me a test of endurance. One glance of a freshly laid cowpat sent me running at full speed for the nearest gate. I certainly wasn't born for a life in the country. Even now, with my senses dulled over time, the smell thing has never got any more bearable. Tom always has the knack of wanting to speak to me during the daily doggy poop pick up exercise in the garden. All he gets is a high-pitched squeal as I frantically shake my head, not daring to take even the smallest of breaths. I can look at most things; am not squeamish at all. Can watch needles go into me, or blood oozing out without so much as a flinch. But one hint of an unpleasant aroma and I am finished. My mum still remembers me flatly refusing to relieve myself anywhere. I was like a camel, able to store up water for up to eight hours at a time rather than enter a less than spotless public lavatory or pee behind a bush. It's like using the bedpan in hospital, it just doesn't seem right. They remember one time having to walk me miles back to town so that I could use a nicer toilet.

* * *

Eventually it was time to leave the sanctuary and safety of the hospital and return to the real world. Being in hospital has sometimes felt like a surreal experience to me. When I was seventeen I was in hospital for a week for an operation on my feet. These days you would be in and out in a day, but not then. I was put on a ward mainly occupied by very sick older people. There was a girl in the next bed to me, can only have been in her very early twenties, quite badly disabled after having a stroke. I had never realised that someone so young could be affected this way and it shook me to the core. Nearly every night someone would lose their battle for life and would be gone by morning. It was shocking to wake up and find yet another empty bed beside you. I remember being stuck on the same page of a book for a whole day, reading it over and over again, so constantly distracted that I couldn't move on to the next chapter. When the nurses said that I could go home if I could make it to the bathroom alone I literally jumped at the chance. I leapt out of bed, ignoring the pain, and ran to the toilet. I didn't want to face another night in that place.

* * *

Nobody can plan their children's future. No one knows what fate has in store for them, or who they will turn out to be. But all the visions I had of the boys growing up the way I had with my own brother were dashed the day we received Connors' diagnosis. The bubble had burst, the visions replaced with uncertainty, speculation and doubt. I felt that both Connor and Tom had been unfairly robbed of a typical childhood.

## 2

## BEFORE THE BOMBSHELL

For the first year of Connors' life we were happily unaware of what was to come. He seemed to be developing normally, as far as we could tell. He was quite quiet, when he wasn't yelling for something, but he ate, drank, crawled, and took some interest in his toys. He didn't seem to be in the crawling stage for very long, preferring to pull himself up and stand instead. When he did walk it was on tip toes for the most part. His height and weight were fine and I'm sure there was plenty of eye contact. He wasn't too keen on having cuddles though; you would have to hold him tight on your knee to get any kind of physical connection. He was much more active than Tom had been and didn't appear to need an awful lot of sleep. He went through phases of sleeping for three to four hours at a time to waking every hour in the night. This was obviously extremely tiring and wearing for the rest of us. I spent many a night downstairs watching Thomas the Tank Engine over and over again. It became a real struggle to function in the daytime, when I hadn't slept for four or five nights in a row.

Tom used to spend his afternoons with me in my office at home. I would wheel his pram next to my desk and with his feet up on the tray, arms folded leisurely behind his head; he would doze happily for hours on end while I worked. Connor, on the other hand, needed a lot more entertaining and seemed to find it difficult to amuse himself, even when surrounded by loads of toys. I wonder now whether he knew what to do with them, or what their purpose was at all. I had kept Tom at home until he was one when he started nursery for a few days a week. I was determined to do the same with Connor so that I could be with him all the time and not miss anything. Not to mention the extortionate nursery fees we have to pay in this country. When I was paying for them both it took nearly all of my salary, and that was only with them in part time. Working from home was ideal though. It meant I could fit the work in around the children, often having to get up early or stay up late into the night to meet a deadline, but I could concentrate when they were asleep so that was fine. I was in charge of preparing monthly management accounts for the Indian branch of an American Medical Company and everything was conducted via e-mail, so thankfully

I didn't need to go to an office. With Franks' heavy travelling schedule I could never have gone out to a full time job and coped with the boys as well. I also had to be around to take him to and from the airport, often at some very unsocial hours. Life was hectic and exhausting, but we were happy. My stepson Guy once commented that our house was 'organised chaos'. It summed us up perfectly.

It was much harder to manage once Connor came along though. I had naively assumed that having two young children wouldn't be that much different to just having the one, but I was very wrong. Luckily Tom was a well-behaved and contented baby so he was easy to care for. I had always joked to people that I would never have another child as good as Tom had been, and my God I was right.

Connor demanded your attention all the time. He didn't like to be left in a room on his own, so I had to constantly cart his travel cot around so that he could play safely, but still see me. When he could stand up he would peer over the edge of his cot, watching as I pottered around the kitchen making dinner. If I ventured anywhere near him, chubby little arms would shoot up in a flash, pleading eyes urging me to pick him up, not for a hug but to make an escape. But he rarely made the usual baby sounds or gurgles you would expect to hear. It was

29

silence or yelling, that was the choice, and it was worth keeping him happy to save your eardrums and your sanity.

He also loved to crash around the house in one of those baby walkers consisting of a seat, a tray to play or eat on, and a frame with wheels on the bottom. He used to hurtle from one room to the next, bashing in to walls and doors. Anything or anyone unfortunate enough to get in his way was unsafe. I lost count of the number of times my feet were run over or ankles bruised by the damn thing. But he loved it and it gave him his freedom and mobility. It also reduced the bouts of screaming. I have loads of photos of him with his head down on the tray, flat out after hours of fun destroying the place.

Apart from throwing up nearly every meal and some vile smelling bowel movements, we were still not one bit concerned with his overall development. I did ponder over how much seemed to come out of him when virtually nothing went in though. I voiced my concerns over his excessive vomiting to our doctor and health visitor but they never seemed to be worried about this. They also never seemed to come up with any solutions either. I was worried that he wasn't getting enough nutrients in to him, but babies throw up a lot, it's quite normal, I was told. We ended up having to prop him up all the time in his little bouncy chair after a bottle, in an attempt to keep some of it down. It was rather frustrating to feed him in the middle of the night only for the whole lot to be regurgitated minutes later. He spent many a night half sat up in his chair next to my bed as I couldn't dare to lie him down in case he threw up and choked. This appeared to work well until he grew so big that he simply couldn't fit into it any longer. He was quite stocky as a baby, we don't know how with the small amount of food that stayed down, but he looked healthy enough, his skin glowed and his energy levels were off the scale. Connor was rarely ill too. Tom had spent his first year at nursery repeatedly catching ear and throat infections. He couldn't seem to resist any bout of sickness that was going round and had more time at home than at school. If I had been going out to work I'd have been fired for all the amount of time I would have needed off to look after Tom. When I was under pressure to finish my accounts my Mum was always kind enough to come over and care for him when he was ill.

It is also a good job that Connor was never sick as he absolutely refuses to take any form of medication. He has a very heightened sense of taste and smell and can always detect even the slightest of changes from a hundred yards away. If we attempt to add even a tiny amount of medicine to his drinks he knows about it. He takes one sip then flatly refuses to go near it again, flinging the cup back at you in utter disgust. You even then have to wash out the cup in front of him to show it has gone before he will go anywhere near that same container. We always made sure he wasn't even in the same room when trying to disguise a dose of paracetamol so he had no way of knowing what was coming but it never once worked. He is able to detect it in anything, even if we make his blackcurrant juice stronger. If reincarnated as an animal in another life he would make an excellent sniffer dog for the Police!

On one occasion, when he was younger, he was sick at school and the nurse kindly offered to help, knowing how hard it was for me to get anything in to him on my own. We cornered him in her office, me trying to keep him still and prise open his mouth whilst she held the spoon. As was inevitable, we both ended up caked in sticky liquid with not a drop having been actually swallowed. Connor was distraught and it took him about twenty minutes to calm down. I drove home in a terrible state, with my fingers glued to the steering wheel. I was annoyed with myself for distressing him so badly, I should have known better than to have tried at all. I have also tried using a syringe with similar disastrous results. I can recall only one single time when he was really poorly with a very high temperature, and he relented enough to drink some juice laced with paracetamol, I think he was so ill that he didn't realise what it was.

His first year passed by with the usual madness of having two children under the age of three. He was still very active and alert, not sleeping for more than a few hours at a time, but I figured that he was just different from how Tom had been, and there was nothing untoward that set the alarm bells off ringing. Not long after he turned one, we made the decision to send him to nursery for a few days a week. As Tom attended there already, Connor was pretty familiar with most of the staff and the building, so it should be less of a shock to the system. Never the less, he yelled each morning for the first few weeks until he settled in. I don't think he ever loved going, but eventually realised there wasn't much choice and tolerated the situation. They noticed he wouldn't eat much and preferred to play in isolation from the other children but this was not that uncommon at such an early age. He eventually outgrew the baby room and was moved on to the toddler room.

I think he was around one and a half to two years old when the teachers started to notice he was acting differently from the rest of the class. They were all about the same age in the room, so it wasn't hard to tell that something was amiss. The children were starting to talk properly and played well together, happy to engage with each other and join in the group activities. They gave the staff good eye contact and always reacted when their names were called. Connor seemed disinterested in all of this. Still preferring solitary play, and becoming increasingly agitated if anyone tried to play alongside him or touch the toy he had hold of. Every time they tried to get his attention they failed miserably. He didn't react or turn his head if they said his name when he couldn't see their face. The staff were becoming increasingly worried that there may be a serious impairment of his hearing. The manager called me in, and she said, as sensitively as she could, that they thought Connor might be deaf. I was adamant that he wasn't, after all I knew him better than anyone, and I was positive that he could hear us. I suggested instead that he was probably ignoring them, so engrossed in his activity that he didn't want to waste time on someone else. He didn't see the point in lots of human contact at that time; he was more than happy being on his own. He didn't feel the need, or know how to share his feelings, desires or emotions. He was content to live alongside us, in a world of his own. Don't get me wrong, we got lots of interaction from him, but it was always on his terms. If Connor wanted something he was sure to let you know about it, often by yelling at the top of his voice. He used others to achieve his goals and requirements. If he enjoyed a certain game or toy he didn't see the point in conveying this enjoyment to anyone else. Opposedly, if he took offence to something he could make himself abundantly clear, usually very, very loudly indeed. I often pointed out birds in the trees or planes flying overhead but he looked blank, as if he couldn't see them at all.

Anyway, the nursery persisted and I agreed to take him for tests. We were sent to a clinic, an environment he has always hated with a passion, for a hearing test. Connor has never been comfortable in strange surroundings unless he is allowed to run free and explore. To be shut in an unfamiliar room, even if I was there too, was a step too far for him. On the first visit he spent the whole time either crying underneath the table or hammering hard on the door, desperate to escape. My repeated attempts to calm him and get him to sit on my knee were futile. In the end we gave up and the health workers suggested waiting a month or so then trying again. The second visit was marginally better. After ten to fifteen minutes under the table he crawled out onto my knee and I held on tightly. With one woman in front of him attempting to interest him in some toys, the other one sat behind us making barely audible noises with different objects at random intervals. As I clung on for dear life, struggling to force him to stay sitting down, I had to wonder how scientific this all really was. I assumed they knew what they were doing, as they had been quick to point this out at the first aborted attempt. When I had inquired, in all innocence, as to how, with all the yelling and jumping about he was doing, they could tell whether he was really deaf or just being stubborn, I was immediately put in my place. Of course they knew what they were doing, they were experts after all, was the answer. After about thirty minutes of bells ringing and various squeaks and whistles, it was decided that he had actually turned his head slightly in reaction to the sounds. The verdict was in, and the conclusion was that he was, in fact, not deaf at all. If I'd been listened to in the first place he, and I, could have been spared the trauma those two visits caused.

This news was understandably a relief to us, but still did not explain his continued reluctance to join in with his peers. He remained at the nursery with all the staff doing their utmost to help him, but he was proving to be rather a handful for everyone.

Even now we weren't overly bothered by his behaviour. We thought he was just a typical, boisterous boy and he would grow out of it and settle down, hopefully. When all the other children were being successfully toilet trained it was decided that Connor was not ready for this yet. Little did I realise then, that this would take until he was seven. When they all sat together for lunch he either ran around or sat staring at his plate, refusing to even attempt a taste of anything. The cook ended up giving him crackers or toast, both of which have remained as his staple diet to this day. When they all played happily in the playground he chose to play alone. Furiously protecting his favourite toys like his life depended on it. There was hell to pay if anyone tried to take them off him. When Christmas came around I was the only parent whose child would not participate in the annual play. He would muck and mess, refusing point blank to put on his designated costume, or get involved at all. One year he broke out of the class early and came into the room with a book. He spent the next hour sitting in the middle of the floor flicking through the pages, oblivious to the festivities going on around him, oblivious to the crowd of adults watching. There were songs, narrations and lots of dancing; he ignored them all. I pretended not to care, but inside I was dying.

I wasn't blind to the circumstances; I knew he was difficult; after all I was the one who lived with him. I was the only parent who spent ten minutes each evening in the car park trying to ram their child into their car seat for the ride home. On one particularly bad night he was in a terrible state. He came out of school very upset for no apparent reason, and it took me ages to wrestle him into the chair. As I pulled out and drove off down the road he escaped out of the safety straps and lay on the floor behind the front passenger seat. I was in a dilemma. The weather was atrocious, the rain battered down heavily, and we were already soaked before we set off after all the commotion in the car park. I figured that I had no chance in hell of getting him back in his seat anyway, so it wasn't worth the effort. I made it home with him now half trapped on the floor, still howling loudly. It took him and me for that matter, ages to calm down. Exactly what had caused that particular tantrum was never to be known. I was also the only parent at the school who had a child of his age who didn't speak.

At around the age of two and a half to three he was referred back to the health care system and social services. There was now an array of different people getting involved. A stream of visitors came to the house, all asking similar questions about him, none being able to answer ours. There were numerous visits to clinics, all of which he detested, all of which were a nightmare for me. He legged around hospitals, trashed health centres, and fought over toys with unsuspecting children. He hated sitting, and he loathed having to wait in designated waiting rooms. He would go berserk whenever we shut the door to a room he was supposed to stay in. He was never left alone with strangers; I was always with him, usually holding his arms in a vice like grip in a futile attempt to stop him from running off. But all my efforts were in vain, he would somehow manage to wriggle free and make a dash for the door. Once out in the corridors he was in heaven; all these places to explore, and long halls to run in. He just could not help himself, he needed to run. It was his passion; an obsession that was impossible to control. He would leg down corridors like his life depended on it, and he was very, very fast. With me, and whatever health professionals we had come to see that day, all chasing madly behind yelling at him to stop he knew he didn't have long. He needed to choose which rooms to visit before we finally found him and hauled him out kicking and screaming. He really wasn't trying to be naughty, just wanted to wander the buildings on his own in his eternal quest for new and exciting things to play with. But many people were uncomfortable with being rudely interrupted in their private offices by this whirlwind of a child who barged his way in, opened drawers and cupboards to see what was in there, and ignored them when they spoke to him. It was decided in the end, that as many meetings as possible should be done at home. They would come to us, instead of us going to them. That was fine by me.

We must have endured at least six months of frequent visits by people who came to analyse Connors' behaviour. He began to feel more like a case study than a little boy. I even found myself carefully watching the patterns and traits he was displaying, rather than enjoying him for who he really was. He had to be monitored constantly as he was pretty destructive and dangerous. As he didn't sleep much, I spent many long days chasing behind him, forever in a state of high alert and panic. He was like a bulldozer; systematically destroying everything he came into contact with, nothing was safe when Connor was around. He would travel round the house trashing each room as he went. As I tidied up the first one he would move on to the next, oblivious to the carnage he left in his wake. No amount of yelling ever did any good. He was deaf to my pleas. As he didn't understand anything we said to him, you couldn't reason with him, or bargain with him. He lived his life on his terms, doing his own thing whenever or wherever he pleased. We had no control over his behaviour; he was like a ticking time bomb that was liable to blow at any opportunity. It was becoming obvious that something was drastically wrong. Each day was a nightmare, every hour a struggle. The only relief I got was when he was at nursery, whilst dreading what stories I would hear about his antics that day when I picked him up. Things got that bad that I stayed at home as much as possible. I had got to the point that I just couldn't face what happened when we went out. Floods of tears became a daily occurrence for me. He was bad enough at home but when out he behaved so much worse. He would escape from me everywhere we went, and destroy rooms in other peoples' houses. I never got the chance to relax as I always had to follow him to stop him wrecking something, or worse still seriously hurting himself. I was totally exhausted all of the time, and desperately in need of someone who knew how to help. The health professionals arrived in their droves, but no one seemed to tell us anything that was of any use, or offered any advice on how to deal with his problems. He was under the care of a speech therapist who, after numerous visits, decided that she couldn't him help because he couldn't speak. We were totally baffled by this, assuming the whole point of speech therapy was to encourage the patient to talk.

Most importantly, no one gave us a reason for the way he was, and if we didn't know what was wrong then we couldn't even start to try to fix it. Not knowing where else to turn we felt trapped. We didn't have much faith in anyone assigned to his care. They were all very nice to us and well meaning, but I didn't feel that we had made much progress at all. I wondered if any of them knew what to do with him. He was around three and a half when he was finally referred to a paediatrician at the hospital. At last we were hopeful of an answer.

# 3

## AND THE WALLS CAME TUMBLING

## DOWN

I think our world fell apart the day we got the definitive diagnosis of autism. Life as we knew it had well and truly ended. For Frank it was immediate, as he knew an awful lot more about the condition than I did. In my case it took a while to sink in…

I will forever remember that day in explicit detail, word for word. Frank was far away in Australia, so I took my Mum along for moral support. We travelled to the hospital chatting happily; I saw this as yet another routine visit, nothing out of the ordinary, nothing to worry about.

It was the usual fight to keep Connor in the waiting room, as these appointments rarely ran on time. After a few trips up and down the corridor in an attempt to keep him amused it was at last time for us to go in. The consultant paediatrician introduced herself, as I hadn't met her before, and we were acquainted with her colleagues, I think there were two of them. My Mum and I sat down and Connor went off to the corner of the room to explore the toys. One of the students went to try and engage him in play whilst we talked to the doctor. We chatted on and off for about thirty minutes, periodically interrupted by me having to jump up and prevent Connor from wrecking the room behind us. Quickly bored with the entertainment on offer, he had discovered the filing cabinets, consulting bed and some sort of hanging mobile suspended above it. He started to bounce excitedly up and down on the hard bed in an attempt to catch on to the mobile. Envisaging it being yanked right out of the ceiling I was only half concentrating on the conversation. She was asking all the usual questions, all the same ones I had repeatedly answered so many times before. Did he line up his toys? Did he flap his hands? Would he chat to you, or could he even talk at all? Was he willing to engage with other children or did he prefer solitary play? There was nothing new, nothing different, no interesting angles that we hadn't explored previously. During this time the doctor appeared to be barely observing Connor who was happily crashing around her office, grabbing everything he could get his hands on. For the last six to nine months I had had to fill in so many forms and questionnaires I was blind on paperwork. There were so many checklists to tick off. Will he look you in the eye? What forms of communication does he use, sign language, pointing, pictures? Is he sensitive to certain types of clothes touching his skin? Is he fussy about what foods he will eat? Over and over again I had answered these questions, the answers always the same. I did wonder if she had even read any of the communications I had sent in before. It all felt so clinical and impersonal, rather similar to completing the checklist for your cars MOT test.

It eventually became obvious that the doctor was actually referring to some of these forms in her file as some references were made to my previous answers, but whether they had been reviewed in preparation for this meeting I was unsure. While we chatted she made some rough notes, about half a page of A4 paper in total over the whole half an hour. At times she interjected the conversation with references to autism, or more specifically the 'autistic spectrum'. Not having ever studied this subject before, and not realising the seriousness of the condition, I didn't really question anything she said. With all the constant interruptions from Connor it was hard to concentrate on much of what was going on.

At the end of the session she pulled out a piece of blank, plain paper. She drew a line horizontally from left to right and motioned us to look at it. She then stated that this line represented the autistic spectrum. The left hand side being mild symptoms of the disorder, and the far right was classed as very severe impairments. I stared at her in silence, wondering what the middle bit stood for. A kind of no man's land filled with uncertainty, misunderstanding, and confusion. I think at this point my mind went blank. There was some talk of where she thought Connor might be on this seemingly enormous scale. She moved her pen backwards and forwards to indicate her predictions. Sort of mild to middle(ish); neither here nor there. It all seemed so inexact and imprecise. I had no clue how to react, or what on earth I was supposed to say. I could feel my temperature rising as my heart beat faster. I had a sudden feeling of needing to get out of there and escape as soon as possible. I attempted to stay focussed as my breathing rate increased, and was blinking rapidly, desperately trying not to show I was about to cry. I just agreed with everything she said. Yes, he was on 'the spectrum', whatever that meant. Yes, he was somewhere in the second quarter, with the constant possibility of shifting either backwards or forwards at any time, for any reason. Yes, he was displaying many of the classic signs of autism, whatever they were. As regards his lack of speech, we were told that some children speak early then stop forever, some start to talk late but will continue to progress. Some just never try to talk at all, forever imprisoned; locked away in their silent, private world. Right now it was anyone's guess what would happen to Connor. As the consultants pen continued to move haphazardly from left to right indicating the numerous possibilities of change on the scale it all began to appear rather scary. He could be here one day, there the next, learn a skill one day then forget it the next. I wasn't sure what I was supposed to do, how I was expected to react, or how I was meant to feel. Eventually, amidst a sea of confusion we managed to escape. We drove home in virtual silence, not wishing to dissect what we had just heard, avoiding the subject completely. There was no follow up appointment arranged, no phone call in two weeks time to see how things were, no opportunity to ask the questions that would undoubtedly pop up over the coming months. That was it, the verdict was in, and it was conclusive.

At this point I was still not too worried. Connor was just Connor to me, whatever label they wanted to put on him, whatever problem they said he had.

Yes he was difficult to look after, extremely challenging in so many ways. In fact, if I was brutally honest, a little swine pretty much all of the time at that age. But he was still the same as he was yesterday, hadn't suddenly developed into a three headed monster overnight. He was still our little boy. I really didn't know what autism was, had never met anyone else with it, and had no clue what to expect. I was blissfully unaware that in that thirty-minute interview, with a mere half a page of random scribbled notes, that doctor had just delivered me one of the worst blows of my entire life. It didn't dawn on me then that I would be plunged into a whirlpool of emotions, and down into the depths of despair. That my life would now include special needs schools, disability living allowance, sign language courses, PECS pictures and respite care. It still didn't register that now, officially, Connor would forever be classed as being disabled by the rest of society and the worst thing was there was absolutely nothing we could do to fix it.

My shock was still to set in, but Franks' reaction to the news was decidedly different. When he called that night to ask how the visit went I managed to remain calm. I repeated, parrot fashion, some of the things the doctor had said about his odd behaviours.

Not knowing how badly the news would hit him, I just blurted it out. So yes, in her view, he has this thing called 'autism'. There was a long silence on the other end of the phone. Sensing trouble, I gulped loudly, and began to feel very nervous. This was obviously not the word he had wanted to hear. I so wished I could take it back; should have played down the situation until he came home, but by now it was far too late. Frank was furious. How dare this doctor, who barely knew Connor, come up with this analogy after only a thirty-minute observation? How dare she label his son this way? I think he was so desperate not to believe it was true. I cried, he yelled, I cried some more. Eventually I put the phone down. Too distraught to even contemplate staying for the remainder of his business trip, he changed his flights and flew home the next day.

* * *

Much later, when we had calmed down and could think rationally, Frank confessed the reason for his initial outburst. His mother had worked as a nurse on special needs wards in a hospital, and used to take him to work with her. These were the wards no one wanted to work in. They were more like an institution for the mentally and physically ill, than a place where people went to recover. These patients had no chance of ever returning to the real world.

They were so badly affected that they were destined to remain there indefinitely, requiring twenty-four hour care until the day they died. He recalled the horror he felt as a very young lad seeing all these terribly disabled children locked away like this. He can remember his mothers' passion and love for these individuals, forgotten and spurned by the rest of society. He didn't recollect them receiving many visits from family members or friends. They were just left there, alone, but for the nurses who cared for them. The one thing he remembered as being common to most of these patients was that they suffered from autism.

* * *

So determined to get a second opinion we demanded to see another paediatrician. This one was way more sympathetic and agreed that we should have been informed in a much gentler and compassionate manner, but the outcome was, sadly, still the same. Even though, by now, the first doctor had very suddenly 'officially' retired, her diagnosis still stood. We were then referred to a psychiatrist. Frank and I went together, under the assumption that we would be discussing Connor, but it turned out to be an analysis of ourselves. The doctor was trying to delve into our minds, and not into his. He was very nice to us, don't get me wrong, but it wasn't what we needed and we left frustrated.

A child psychologist was assigned to us. On her first visit she yet again asked the same questions whilst watching Connor play, again it can't have been for more than an hour or so. She seemed quite optimistic, not too sure whether he was really bad enough to be classed as being on the spectrum at all. By the time she left Frank was ecstatic. This was the news he had been hoping for, a positive lifeline to cling on to. The same woman returned to see us quite soon afterwards. This time the outcome was not so good. In retrospect she had backtracked. Now, in her professional opinion, they were all right. He did indeed have autism. She talked to us about starting the process of obtaining a statement of educational needs. This was essential if he was to secure a place at a special needs school. In her opinion this type of school was his only option. This news was another huge blow for us. Up to then we hadn't even considered the thought that he couldn't attend the same school as his brother. We were left wondering how those few weeks between visits had resulted in such a massive change of direction. How could he have gone from not appearing too bad, to needing intensive specialized teaching within two weeks? I think this was the point where we entirely lost all faith in the system as a whole. We had no clue where to turn to next. We had to continue to deal with the day-to-day pressures of normal life; work commitments; looking after two young children; financial issues etc. On top of this we had to digest, and come to terms with, all that had recently come to light. We started to read up on the condition. There were thousands of articles written, hundreds of websites to visit. It was difficult to decipher which ones were the most useful. Some gave me hope; others shocked me to the core. In many ways it was good to know we weren't alone, there were so many other families facing similar issues. But however comforting this knowledge should have been, it didn't make me feel any stronger or wiser. This was a very scary and confusing time for us, and I could really have done with a huge shoulder to cry on.

For the educational statement to be constructed many people were expected to give their input. There were to be reports written by all those involved in his care, including us. We met regularly with all the separate individuals, but eventually requested a meeting where everyone could be brought together. This was conducted at his nursery school at around 9.30am one particular morning. As I recall there were about six or eight of us expected to attend. Everyone had shown up on time, with the exception of the speech therapist. We all sat there awkwardly exchanging polite conversation. The kind of nonsensical chatter you do with virtual strangers when you are avoiding the real issue at hand. Eventually she turned up about half an hour late, giving some pathetic excuse no one wanted to hear. The discussion now centred on Connor, and each person had the opportunity to give his or her views on his progress. I remember getting quite upset at one point, and fought hard not to lose control. They could all talk about him in the third person, removed from their emotions. He was yet another child on their records, just another file in the drawer. They all had the privilege of going home after a day's work and forgetting all about him. We didn't have that option.

* * *

Time went on and things started to go downhill. He had a few bad accidents at nursery, due to his excessive climbing. We never blamed the staff; in fact they all went out of their way to help as best they could. But, as willing as they were, they weren't trained in managing children like Connor. The manager of his room at the time was given a crash course in one to one teaching methods and was then able to give him some more appropriate tuition during the day. In the end though, it became obvious that he couldn't stay there any longer. He had been happy, but it was time to move on.

In all, it took about six months of yet more meetings and form filling to obtain the educational statement. They made it sound so convoluted and long winded, but realistically it was simply a few bits of paper stating Connors' needs in a school environment. Nothing fancy, nothing scientific, nothing new. Why it needed to take so long is anybody's guess. Now it was time to choose a school. Not that there was much choice available, but still a very important decision to make. It was essential that Connor went to the right place, was surrounded by the right people and, most importantly, was happy and safe.

# 4

## STARTING SCHOOL

Now we had a fresh challenge, to find Connor the right school. It seemed a daunting task, but really there were only a few places to choose from. In the area where we live, when you receive a statement of educational needs, they offer their choice of recommendations. I think there were three to choose between, but it was to be us, as his parents, who would have the final say. We were encouraged to visit them all and then make an informed decision.

We made an appointment and turned up at the first school. We were greeted warmly and ushered in to an office to wait for the head teacher. She was just finishing the morning assembly and would be with us in a few moments. She soon arrived, and after a quick introduction, suggested a tour of the school before we sat down for a chat. Lining the corridors was the usual array of artwork and exhibits all proudly constructed by the pupils. There were some children moving from one class to the next or to the library. All seemed to have varying degrees of communication or physical disabilities. The head made a point of stopping and saying hello to every child we passed and asking how they were that day. Those who were capable of answering did so politely and appropriately. I noted the fact that she knew each and every one of them by their first names and had a story to tell about them all. She had clearly made a point of really getting to know the pupils; they were not just a name on the register to her. They were all treated with the utmost respect and compassion and she was genuinely interested in their welfare. This, I thought was a lovely touch, you rarely see that in a mainstream setting. We observed some class lessons and saw a physical education session outside before retiring back to the school office. The head asked some questions about Connor and indicated that he would be very welcome there if that is what we decided. The one thing she said that stuck with me the most was that all the children could learn good manners. Regardless of colour, religion, class, nationality, or disability, the majority of the children could be made to learn the simple lesson of being polite and courteous to fellow human beings. This, I thought, was a wonderful gift to give them for their journey through life. Maybe some other schools would benefit from enforcing this lesson. We thanked her for her time and went on our way. Positive, for the fact, that everyone there had seemed so lovely. Devastated inside that our own son needed to attend a school such as this.

When we arrived at the second school we were immediately greeted at the door by the head herself. I think we had a short chat before heading off down the main corridor towards the hall and classrooms. Again, the walls were lined with some very creative and imaginative art. It was clear that the children took pride in their work. She showed us around and we met some of the staff and pupils. I was initially taken aback at some of the severe disabilities that many of them had. There were more children with obvious physical problems than there had been at the first school. A few were so bad that they needed to be tightly strapped in to specially adapted wheelchairs for their own safety. Some struggled to walk and were helped by the use of Zimmer frames, more commonly used by the elderly. One tiny little boy had a breathing tube in his neck and an oxygen tank permanently strapped to the back of his wheelchair. Some wore helmets to avoid a head injury when they fell over, or threw themselves against a wall. It was saddening to see so many young people having to suffer these terrible problems. They didn't deserve the hand they had been dealt in this life. But there was one thing they all seemed capable of doing, one common trait that ran throughout. They all came across as being happy. This we took to be a wonderful sign, the staff were obviously doing a great job. When we got back to the heads' office we all sat down and she asked us if we had any questions. Already having learned a lot about the place as we'd walked round, I didn't have much else to ask. Frank and I looked at each other in silence for a few seconds. We only had one thing to say, and I think we said it virtually in unison. "When can he start?"

So that was that. Why we had chosen the second school over the first we weren't too sure. Both seemed great and appropriate for Connor, but we just felt he would be happier in the one we had picked. It was such a relief that we had found somewhere we felt he would settle. It would be another story as to how he would react when he came here, as he is extremely unpredictable, but we were content with our choice. We never did go to see the third school. Having already chosen the second, it seemed a pointless exercise, and we didn't want to waste anyone's time. We had also been advised that this setting was home to some even more severely disabled children and we simply couldn't face any more sadness. Ironically though, that third school happened to be situated in the same road as our house, but we were still confident the correct place had been picked to suit Connors' needs.

* * *

We decided to move him after the May half term holiday and let him hopefully settle in before the break for summer. We were in two minds as to whether to leave it until September; this second option appealed to me the most, as it meant he would not be off for the whole six weeks. As even one week at home with him was bad enough, I dreaded the thought of six. However, after two accidents occurred at the nursery, within days of each other, we thought it best to move him. We never blamed the staff; he had been climbing yet again and had fallen, resulting in some nasty deep gashes to his legs. It was his own fault, but we had to wonder how closely he had been monitored. He needed to be protected from himself and we were sure that the school knew how to manage this.

* * *

Starting school can be scary for any child, and equally traumatising for their parents. I remember Toms' first day, having to leave him screaming and distraught in the classroom, and force myself to walk away. I was trying desperately not to let him see that I was crying too. I had thought that having been to both nursery and pre-school then he would be reasonably prepared for this, and was quite taken aback at his reaction. I ran out of the grounds and reached the gate before daring to look back. I felt so sorry for him, so little and alone, I wanted to rush back in, scoop him up and take him home. Obviously, this wasn't allowed, so I drove home through a sea of tears. It took a while, but as predicted, he soon settled in and was fine. He is now a confident and well-respected member of his school community.

Connor starting school was a completely different story. Even coming to terms with the fact that he couldn't go to a mainstream school proved difficult for us at first. I had so hoped that he would end up at the same place as Tom. I envisaged standing at the gate in the mornings waving them off as they ran happily down to the playground. At home time they would rush out, bursting to tell me all about their day. They would drown each other out as they fought to tell their news first. There would be endless tales about mutual friends, vile school dinners, and who hit who in the yard at break. There would be excitement about the next disco that was coming up soon, and school photos taken of the two of them together. The realisation that all this was never going to happen hit like a hammer blow, and took me a long while to accept. One of my lowest points was not long after he had been diagnosed. I vaguely remember spending the Christmas holidays totally distraught. I was still unable to speak about his autism without breaking down, and I recall spending those whole two weeks in floods of tears. I think we all reacted differently to the news. I fell apart and wasn't much use to anyone for a while. I just managed to get through each day, grateful for bedtime when I could get lost in the unreality of my dreams. I couldn't cope with my own emotions, let alone worry about anybody else's. It probably would have helped us both enormously if Frank and I could have sat down and discussed matters more openly, but I just cried at the mere mention of Connors' name. Frank threw himself in to researching the subject. He studied everything from autistic traits and possible links to vaccines, to effects from certain food groups. He found American medical institutes claiming to change peoples' lives and 'recover' them from autism. He was desperate for answers and a potential cure. Luckily Tom was too young to understand most of what was going on so he didn't have to feel the pain we did. I tried to hide my stress from him as much as possible and attempted to carry on for his sake. I am so glad that we had Tom before Connor. Having him to look after has kept me sane and focussed, as he was always there to divert me away from being too down or depressed. Life had to go on for Toms' sake, no matter how low I sank.

* * *

My reality of Connors' first day at school was so far derived from what I had envisaged. I had to put him on a bus with two strangers, the driver and the escort. I couldn't explain to him where he was going or why. He didn't really speak then, and had no concept what the word 'school' meant. All he knew was that he was being put in an unfamiliar vehicle with strange people going god knows where, and he didn't know if he was ever coming home again. You couldn't reassure him by saying "see you later" or "mummy will be here when you get home", he understood very little of what we said. All he knew was that we were sending him away. The escort was a lovely girl aged around eighteen, and she always did her best to make these journeys as enjoyable as possible for Connor. I recall that very first day as being one of the better ones. As he didn't know where they were going, he was not too reluctant to co-operate. I made sure he was safely strapped into his seat, and waved as the bus trundled off down the road. I went back in and closed the door feeling somewhat deflated. I was relieved we hadn't had to endure any hysterics, but gutted by the fact that I couldn't take him to school myself. I felt I was missing out on this very important step in his life.

The next day didn't go so well. Now, having cottoned on to where the bus would take him, he decided to resist. After all, he had been there for one day, why the need to go again? This time there was murder. He wouldn't even get dressed, and he quickly associated the uniform was linked to his final destination. Unfortunately, this morning drama was to last for many years to come. There were the odd days when he decided to behave, but mostly not. I tried to be sneaky and not show him his clothes until breakfast was over. He ate so little anyway; he couldn't afford to miss out on the only meal of the day he actually liked. It would then be a half hour fight to have a wash and wrestle on his uniform. The mere sight ignited the onset of hysteria. He was unable to dress himself at all at that stage, so I would have to pick up his feet in turn to attempt to get a pair of underpants over his nappy. A chase would then ensue throughout the house with him trying to dodge me at every turn. He would fight and squirm and struggle, whilst yelling at the top of his voice. When I was lucky enough to get on a pair of shorts and a polo shirt, more often than not they would be off again within seconds. It took him a very long time to learn to dress himself; the undressing came naturally. I was grateful that the school didn't insist on a shirt and tie; we'd have been there all day. Often the bus would arrive while all this lunacy was still in full swing. Luckily they were well used to it and more than happy to wait. This madness was then followed by numerous trips back up stairs to get whatever he wanted to take that day. He would set his heart on one particular thing, usually a toy, video or DVD. If he couldn't find the exact item there was trouble. No amount of persuasion helped. No chance of accepting an alternative. I would end up emptying toy boxes all over the floor frantically searching out the required object, there was no way he was going to leave quietly without it. At one point he was taking a whole carrier bag full of videos every day, even the teachers asked if we could limit him to one, as things were getting out of hand. With the required toy secured safely in his bag, he agreed to leave the house. Once he was successfully out of the door the next problem began. If he didn't fancy school that day he refused point blank to sit in his seat. He would run up and down the bus and climb the pole at the front. If we didn't catch him in time he would curl up in a ball under a seat and refuse to come out. After a few failed attempts by the escort to gently coax him out I had to step in. I would drag him out and shove him forcibly into his designated chair. Sounds rather cruel I know, and I hated to do it, but no amount of pleading was ever going to work. It was then a case of wresting on the seat belt before he went stiff and wouldn't bend in the middle. There were so many starts to the day like this I lost count. I would jump off the bus and walk up the path with tears of frustration stinging my eyes. I couldn't understand why he insisted on putting himself, and me, through this trauma, day in day out. Certain days he was so bad that I actually rang the school later to check he was okay. They were always quick to reassure me. He had calmed down during the journey and had arrived happily singing to himself or laughing loudly. This was comforting to know, but in a way annoying too. Was the way he acted each morning just for my benefit? Did he think that if he yelled for long enough he would get his own way and be allowed to stay at home? We never dared do this, imagining the disastrous consequences if he learnt we might give in. Given the chance, Connor would quite happily stay at home every day, never to step foot in school again.

He has no idea that they are trying to help him and educate him, so that he has the chance of a better future. What child of a young age can see that anyway?

* * *

Before Connor started school my Mum and I had gone for a visit. We spent an hour or so in the reception class he was set to join. What hit me most was how empty the room was. No pictures adorned the walls; no toys or books filled the shelves. The whole place was bare, apart from the items needed for the activity that was being currently worked on. There were only locked cupboards, clear tables, and doors with high handles and bolts at the top. It seemed so sparse and uninviting. My first thought was that Connor would be really bored here. It felt like a prison cell and I was shocked by the sight. I have since learned why it has to be like this. For a start, some of the children drag down the pictures and eat them, together with the 'blue-tack' that was holding them up. None of them could focus on a lesson if there were any distractions within easy reach. After each short session of learning the cupboards were unlocked and they could choose their reward. This might be reading a book, playing with a favourite toy, or ten minutes computer time. This made total sense of course, and is proven to be very effective. They would work better if they knew a treat was coming afterwards. With most of the children having a very limited concentration span, they had no hope of achieving anything if they could see something of interest across the classroom.

* * *

So Connor started school after the bank holiday, and eventually settled into some kind of routine. He only had about six weeks or so to go before they broke for summer.

# 5

## A VERY SCARY MONSTER

According to Connor we have a very scary monster living among us. It is big, yellow, and very hairy, with huge, sharp, sparkling white teeth and a long wet floppy tongue. It patrols the halls in the dead of night, seeking out its prey, searching every dark corner and crevice, ready to pounce in a second at the slightest thing.

In reality, it is our beloved four-year-old Labrador retriever called Toffee, hunting out a slipper or a used sock discarded at bedtime. She is a very generous dog, obsessed with giving presents to those she loves. In fact almost any unsuspecting visitor to the house will be happily greeted with a flip-flop or a slipper (as these are kept by the front door, handy to grab at a moments notice). If they are very lucky they may be presented with a soggy bone or worse still a recently chewed tug toy. They are then expected to get hold of one end and engage in a wrestling match. Many people back off at this point, not too keen to grab a potentially very saturated piece of rope.

It is lovely to be woken first thing with a wet slipper slapped across your face. It is then a race against time to get it back before it ends up too wet to wear, I think mine go in the wash more often than my jeans. If you are lucky enough to get it back in time then this is no problem. She gives in graciously, pads off, and is back within seconds with another. We often end up with all the slippers hidden under the bed covers by the time we get up. If you have been silly enough to leave discarded socks on the floor then these will also suffice as an early morning alarm call. They are more fun as she can fit nearly a whole sock in her mouth in one go, making it much more challenging to retrieve it. One of us has to prise open very strong jaws, then whoever drew the short straw, usually me, has to reach in and unhook the material from around each tooth. This has to be done rather swiftly before the window of opportunity literally snaps sharply shut. There is then only one other option to get it back, a snack from the doggy biscuit tin. Nothing inedible is worth holding on to when a tempting tasty treat is on offer instead. The morning post and free newspapers are equally useful as a means to gain an extra bone or two. If you don't realise they have been abducted quite soon though you can often end up with some very soggy letters. I once had to unpeel half a letter from the Inland Revenue from the roof of her mouth. The other half was never to be seen again. Luckily no new credit cards have suffered the same fate just yet.

The decision to get a dog was made during the summer when Connor was six. We weren't really sure what his reaction was going to be, but we knew that in time he would grow to accept it invading his home. The dog was really not for Connor anyway, his brother had been asking for a pet for a long time and I finally relented and promised to think about it. Once we had all decided that some kind of pet would be good for Tom, it would give him something else to focus on when he was fed up trying to cope with Connor, the hardest decision was what type of pet we were going to go for. Knowing full well that I would be the one left to look after it for the majority of the time, I felt I should have more say than anyone else. I was adamant that it was to be a small, self-cleaning, preferably caged animal that would need very little intervention during the day whilst we were all working or at school. Possibly a hamster or gerbil as they would be very easy to maintain, wouldn't need walking, and would be easy to re house temporarily if we were going away on holiday. I definitely didn't want fish. I couldn't see myself cleaning out a smelly tank, and hadn't even managed to keep my niece's goldfish alive for one week. Imagining the scenario of Connor tipping the whole lot on to the living room floor, climbing on top of the tank or worse still into it, or attempting to catch the fish with his bare hands, had put me off for life. Everyone thought the hamster idea was a bad one. Jayne had had them as a young child and remembered them biting a lot; they didn't have a very long life span either. Rabbits weren't even a consideration; I preferred a house pet, so I suggested a cat. Having lived with them most of my life anyway, I was relatively confident that I was capable of looking after one. Frank however didn't want a cat, having always been a dog person, so I was unanimously outvoted. A dog it was. Tom, of course, was ecstatic. I was dreading the thought of what I'd let myself in for.

I was not a complete novice when it came to the world of dog ownership. We had already had a dog, for the year leading up to Tom being born. Frank had recalled having a number of different dogs during his childhood. One in particular had stood out among the rest, a large male Springer spaniel called Major. Frank had fond memories of Major.

He remembered a calm, quiet, sensible dog. Knowing absolutely nothing about breeds of dog at that time I was more than happy to go along with it. We visited a breeder with loads of cute and cuddly looking puppies staring back at us with large, sad eyes. It was horrible to see them all barking like crazy and scratching at the cage doors, desperate to escape. The staff seemed very caring towards the dogs, but it was obviously a very lucrative money making business. In hindsight, I suppose, we should have just walked away. We have been advised now that you should see at least one of the parents before buying a puppy, rescue dogs excluded of course, but we weren't aware of this then. So we went ahead and bought a lovely looking, cute, friendly, male Springer. 'Major the second' had arrived. We settled him in at home and Frank left on a business trip the next morning. I was alone for the first time with an animal I knew absolutely nothing about. Okay, I thought, I can cope; it can't be that hard to control this tiny little ball of fluff. Oh my God, how wrong I was.

With not yet having had children, I hadn't much experience of sleep deprivation. After three nights of lying on a cold kitchen floor, a wet tongue down my ear, I had had enough. The next night I left him to howl himself to sleep. I was the only person in the house anyway, so there was no one else to disturb. He went quiet after a while, and totally exhausted I fell in to a very deep sleep, unaware that my kitchen was systematically being destroyed downstairs. Sadly this destruction was to continue. He hated being left alone at all, even for a short time. He wasn't a fussy dog where food was concerned though, everything that stood still was deemed edible. Anything on hand was worth getting your teeth into, wooden skirting boards, chair legs, kitchen cupboards, plants, shoes, his dog bed and bedding. Even the walls themselves were not spared. Not content with just chewing the legs off our kitchen table, he stood up and ate the top of it too. We still have that table for the kids to play on, and I still remember Major when I see the bite marks.

Unfortunately, this was only the tip of the iceberg. As it transpired, Major had some massive flaws in his genetic makeup. Springer's are well known for their boundless energy and zest for life. Every time we dared to let him off his lead he legged it, big time. He refused to come back, no amount of yelling his name ever worked. The worst day was when Frank had taken him out for a walk on the beach. He phoned me to say that the dog was nowhere to be seen, and that he was rapidly sinking in the mud. The water was far out and he had walked across the bay to try and find him. The mud was now well past his knees and he couldn't get out. With no one close enough to shout to for help he rang me. In a state of wild panic I jumped in the car and flew off down the road. The beach was only a ten minute drive away but it felt like an eternity. I had no idea just how far Frank was from civilisation, no idea when the tide might turn, and no idea where to start looking. I ran across the road from the car park, frantically looking for anyone I could ask for help. I felt my heart thumping hard in my chest. This was a huge expanse of open sand and I had no clue what I was going to do. Just as I felt I was going to lose it, I saw a very muddy, and I think very relieved Frank walking towards me. He had somehow managed to pull himself free and the look on his face said it all. We never needed to have the conversation as to what might have happened that day. We were both fully aware of the alternative outcome to this situation. Eventually, as they usually do, the dog found the way back by himself. Having spent a few blissful hours chasing sea gulls and getting extremely dirty, he decided enough was enough. We dragged him home, smelly and tired, to a bath and bed.

After this episode I was now very wary of letting him off the lead when I was alone. Being such an energetic dog though, walking on the lead was just not enough. He would pull me along, twisting and turning, constantly wrapping the rope around my legs. You couldn't really call it a walk, more like a fast jog. I got sick to death of being yanked down the road. I kept pulling him back, saying heel, making him wait a few seconds then trying again, but it never worked. I had always envisaged having a dog that would sleep contentedly at my feet whilst I worked. We would enjoy long happy strolls together on warm sunny afternoons. I pictured a dog that would sit by my side in the evenings, snoring softly, whilst I watched the TV. It would be a great friend and loyal companion, especially as Frank had to work away so much of the time. I hadn't, however, envisaged a dog that destroyed everything, attacked me whenever the phone rang, escaped at every opportunity, and never seemed to get the hang of toilet training. I hadn't envisaged Major. He was in control, not us.

In desperation, I sought out a dog obedience school; it was run by a police dog handler at a local farm. Perfect. They would be able to teach me the skills I needed to control this lunatic. I didn't fully blame Major for the way he was; it was probably a combination of factors. I was sure that possible inter breeding, not getting enough exercise off lead, and my lack of doggy knowledge, were all in part to blame for his behaviour. I needed to learn to be strong and not let him beat me. Of course, he was well behaved at the classes, obediently walking up and down to heel, looking like butter wouldn't melt. The minute we got home all the work was forgotten and he turned back in to his old self.

By the time I was due to have Tom, we had had Major for just over a year. I was very worried that I wouldn't handle a baby with this crazy dog. I was also very worried for the baby's safety. Major liked nothing better that violently shaking and destroying his toys. I wondered whether he was the kind of dog who could be trusted around a small child. I would of course be careful not to leave them alone together, but it was a chance we just couldn't take. We made the sad decision that he had to go.

The police decided that he would make a great sniffer dog, so we packed up his things and waved goodbye. In spite of how difficult he had been we were still sorry to see him leave. At least we were comforted by the thought that he was going to a better place. A place where he would get tons of exercise, be well looked after, and be happy. As it transpired though, even the police couldn't control him.

A few weeks later we got a phone call to say that he had been chasing sheep and they didn't feel they could trust him. He wasn't police dog material after all. We had to go to the dog / horse centre and pick him up.

We were in a dilemma. We had Tom now and didn't fancy his chances against a huge, manic animal. We needed to find another home for Major. After about a week of him being back with us I couldn't handle it. We booked him in to a kennel whilst we decided what to do. Luckily there was a Springer Rescue Centre not far from where we live. They agreed to help us and within weeks had found him a new, more appropriate, home. A couple had lost their dog and were looking for a new one, they were fully aware of the needs of this type of breed, and didn't have young children. Major was re homed, again, and we heard that he had settled in well. At last we were at peace. He was happy, we were happy, and Tom was safe.

* * *

After all this, it was only understandable that I was rather nervous and hesitant about getting another dog. Major had put me off for life, and with Connor to cope with, I felt I had enough on my plate already. But we had made a promise to Tom, so that was that. I spoke to a few parents at the school gate and as luck would have it the breeder where they got their dogs from had a new litter of five-week old Labrador puppies. The mother dog had had twelve in all, seven male, five female, and all yellow. I decided that I wanted a girl; I lived in a house of men already and fancied the thought of some female company, even if it wasn't of the human form. Besides, I had had a male dog before, and apart from them tending to grow larger than the females, I didn't fancy the image of it sitting at the school gate, legs akimbo, doing a full scale wash of its private bits. It had to be a girl, or nothing.

As it happened, there were three females left to choose from. We made an appointment to visit straight away, and decided we better all go together as this choice would affect us all. Poor Connor was traumatised even before we got through the door. As we were trying to coax him out of the car, he is often wary of visiting strange places, two puppies from a previous litter came bounding up to meet us. They were only around six months old, but to him they were very large, and very scary. Luckily the owners came out and shooed them away, enabling us to persuade Connor to enter the house. There were three tiny puppies asleep in a huge metal cage in the corner of the kitchen. Tom and I went over and sat on the floor, while the lady who breeds them opened the cage and gently prodded them into consciousness. She lifted each one out and plonked them on our knees so we could decide which of the three we might choose. As we sat stroking the dogs, Connor was getting more and more agitated. Not interested in the puppies at all, he wanted to escape out of the room to go and explore. Obviously, being in a stranger's house, we couldn't let him do that, so after a lie down protest and plenty of yelling he had to be escorted back to the car in disgrace. We quickly decided that it was a tossup between two of the dogs. Neither Tom nor I could choose, so Frank decided to pick the one with the blue ink on the end of its tail, as opposed to the one with the red. To be accepted as a member of our family you had to support Everton, Franks' favourite football team, hence the choice of name – Toffee.

At eight weeks old we were allowed to bring her home, and for once I was organised. I had bought a bed, bedding, bowls, food, and plenty of toys. I had even got a book to educate myself in caring for Labradors. I felt better prepared this time, but still very worried. I was going to have this animal to look after all day; every day, for the next fourteen years or so, and I wasn't sure I was ready for such a commitment. I hardly slept the night before, tossing and turning, waking up every half hour in a state of panic, and feeling physically sick. This was ridiculous, I had been less nervous the night before my heart operation. I was relieved when morning came. Tom and I set off with a cardboard box containing a blanket and a fluffy blue hippo. I drove her home slowly and carefully, as if we had a newborn baby in the back seat, luckily it wasn't too far. Tom sat next to her to ensure she didn't attempt an escape from the box. As it happened, she was so laid back she fell asleep and didn't even wake up when we carried her into the house. After a few hours hiding behind the couch, she ventured out to explore her new surroundings.

When Connor came home from school that afternoon he was in for a shock. He was not impressed one little bit. It had been bad enough having to visit them, but why now was this horrible, furry, wild creature in his own house? He named her 'the scary monster' and ran away every time she went anywhere near him. He spent those first three weeks living in total fear of what she might do. Each time he entered the kitchen, he would jump up on the work surfaces, so his feet couldn't be anywhere near her. He climbed on anything he could find – the dinner table, chairs, settee, cooker, and fridge, even up the door frame. Anything, rather than set foot on the floor where you could potentially be attacked by a vicious, man-eating predator. Even if she so much as looked at him he would emit a high-pitched squeal and pole vault over the baby gate into the safety of the hall. His reaction amused us intensely; Toffee was the cutest, cuddliest, fluffiest bundle of fur you could possibly imagine. Connor acted like we had a two headed, six-eyed, blood-sucking alien lurking among us.

\* \* \*

It took a number of months, but eventually he accepted the fact that she was here to stay. It was still a long time though, before he relaxed enough to stroke her, or allowed her to sit next to him. He liked her better when she was sleeping, and would sneak over for a closer look, careful not to wake her up. It has helped enormously that she is such an easy going, happy, and contented dog. I swear that from day one she instinctively knew that she needed to be calmer with Connor. She would go wild when Tom was around, jumping up at him and chasing him round the house, play fighting and biting, as young puppies tend to do. But she never tried to do that to Connor, she seemed to sense that he didn't like that kind of interaction. She even acts like his protector when we all go for walks together. When he runs ahead of us, which is all the time, she runs with him and stays close by until we catch up. If we lose sight of them in the park we have learnt not to shout for Connor; that is futile. Instead, you call the dogs name and a head will immediately appear out of nowhere, from behind a tree or rock, we know then where to find them both.

Even now, years down the line, Connor still acts like he doesn't really care that much about the dog. He will shove her out of the way if she is in his path, or sometimes give a quick stroke in passing as she brushes past his legs. He tends to treat her in a similar fashion to the way he treats the rest of us. He knows we are all members of his family, and he likes to know where everyone is, but he doesn't need you to be in his line of sight. As long as you are around when he needs you, that is enough. When he gets home from school he bangs on the door, excited to be back. Not particularly eager to see us though, just to play with his favourite toys, watch the TV, or bounce on the trampoline. There are no big hugs, no kisses, no hello's as he barges his way in. You are lucky to get even a fleeting glance as he rushes past on his way upstairs, leaving a trail of discarded uniform behind in his wake.

There have been a few instances though, when he has shown his affection for Toffee. I took her into school one day for the children to meet her. We visited each classroom and left Connors class until the end, as he would immediately assume it was home time if he caught sight of me. All the children loved her; even the ones who couldn't walk or talk seemed to take great pleasure in feeling the softness of her fur. Some of them were a bit rough, pulling at her tail and ears, but she didn't turn a hair, just sat there and let them. She would make a great 'pets for therapy' dog, visiting the sick and elderly in hospital. When we finally reached Connor's room the whole class surrounded her, all wanting to pat her first. Connor waded in, took the lead off me, and said "take Toffee home now". I think he wanted to make the point that she was his dog, and no-one else's.

There was also one very touching time I recall. I walked past the living room door one day to see Toffee lying on the settee, with Connor lying next to her. He was resting his head on her back with his arms folded underneath his head, and was spread out, legs casually crossed at the ankle. They both looked so contented watching TV together, like the best of friends. I crept away, not wishing to disturb them and ruin the moment.

* * *

Despite my initial trepidation, getting Toffee has been one of the best things we could have done. She fits in so well, joins in everything we do, and loves being part of the family. She has cured Connor of his dog phobia, forced us to do some much-needed exercise, and is a great diversion for Tom. Most importantly, she is a wonderful friend to us all.

# 6

## THE DANGER ZONE

Most toddlers go through a destructive phase in their early lives. From the moment they discover how to crawl around, nothing within reach is safe anymore. You hide away those items that have either any financial or sentimental value. Prized possessions and breakable ornaments are banished to high shelves or lockable cupboards, until such a time when it is deemed safe enough to reinstate them in their rightful place. Connor however, has never grown out of his wrecking ability. In fact, this is an area he has excelled in greatly. There isn't much left in our house that hasn't suffered to some degree at Connors' hands.

We are finally only now attempting to re hang some of the curtains in our home. We spent years with nearly none up at all, only the front living room ones survived as both the rail and the hooks are made of metal as opposed to the usual plastic. They are actually annoyingly noisy each time you open or close them, but to be fair they are the only ones that have stood up to years of abuse from Connor. Not content with just trashing the curtains themselves, many of the rails got smashed down too. He would gather the material in his arms and then jump off the windowsill, swinging wildly like a monkey from one side to the other. We would find broken hooks strewn across floors and the curtains bravely hanging on by the odd remaining hook that had somehow miraculously survived. In the end it was easier to just take them down, in the hope that they could be reinstated one day. I was concerned that he would really hurt himself, but he never did.

It really is an obsession of his to jump and bounce and climb up things, he just can't stay still. It's a real compulsion that he has absolutely no control over, and a real passion that he loves immensely. He gets so over excited at times that it seems to be his way of releasing all the energy he has stored up inside. We can't stop him, he needs to do it, so the best we can do is try to ensure his environment is as safe as possible. I had hoped that these huge energy levels would diminish with time, but as yet there doesn't seem to have been much progress in this area. At best I think that some of his worst behaviours have been modified, but only to be replaced by something equally as dangerous.

We never did have many ornaments or vases in the house but most of those we did own have long since been attacked and destroyed by our wild child. We once had a lovely statue of the Greek goddess Aphrodite that had been carefully carried all the way home by Frank from a business trip. It hadn't cost anything as it had been given to us as a gift, but we really liked it and it had pride of place in our back living room. To protect it while I decorated, it was moved upstairs to a high shelf in the bedroom. Connor decided it would be fun to climb up and launch himself off the shelf and onto the bed. Unfortunately the statue came too, missing the bed it smashed to pieces on the floor. Sadly even a whole tube of superglue couldn't save it, it was way beyond repair. It ended up in the bin, along with all the other broken things he has ruined over the years.

He also loves to walk along the tops of radiators and throw himself off onto the couches in the living room. If there happens to be anything hanging on the wall within easy reach, then this gets grabbed in the process. We have lost a few pictures and a large mirror this way, them having been literally ripped off the walls, together with the picture hooks and the plaster surrounding them.

Door hinges are our biggest problem at the moment. As Connor is always in such a rush the doors get flung open to their widest capacity then slammed shut hard. The whole conservatory shudders with the force and we have lost count of the number of times the hinges have had to be mended. If he carries on like this he will eventually smash them off altogether, resulting in a very expensive problem for us. We are constantly telling him to be careful, and I show him by opening and closing the doors gently myself, but this message just doesn't seem to sink in at all. You can't explain the consequences of his actions to Connor; he has no clue what you are saying and no idea what can happen.

In Connors' opinion life is far too short to sit still or relax for a second; there is absolutely no time to waste. He can't even sit still to eat, preferring to carry his food around with him for the most part. We feel we have no option but to let him be and just monitor his movements to ensure his safety, but even that has proved impossible on some occasions in the past. Short of tying him to a chair or drugging him senseless we have no control, and we are obviously prepared to do neither of these things. I have to admit though the thought of drugging him into a calmer state did tempt us to try it just the once.

It was years ago, when the thought of yet another horrendous trip to Spain got the better of me. It was back when he was impossible to cope with at the airport and I begged the doctors to help us. I couldn't stand the thought of yet another hellish journey. We were given a medicine that taken in the right dose should just take the edge off. Not put him to sleep, but make him calm and easier to control. I was really excited that this would work and slipped a spoonful into his drink for the drive to the airport. Of course I should have known better than to try and trick him. After one sip he flung the cup down in disgust, refusing to drink another drop. I had no choice but to pour it away and show him it had gone; this was even before we had got in the car. Whether he was angry at what I had tried to do or very excited at going away we will never know, but he was wilder and more bad tempered than ever that day. Supposedly it was a strong drug and we wondered if that tiny sip had been enough to set off an adverse reaction. We threw the rest away, deciding it was safer never to try it again.

From the moment he learned to walk, he learned how to climb. He was out of his cot and over the baby gates at a much younger age than Tom had been. I had wanted to use the gates as a way of keeping him in his room at night. At least then I knew where he was and more importantly, could limit the level of destruction he could get up to, but in the end it was too unsafe. If the gate collapsed whilst he was standing on it then he would get badly hurt, so we were forced to remove them much earlier than we had hoped. He very quickly learned to climb anything and everything, and spent most of his time indoors with his feet off the ground. He would climb onto the mantelpiece above the fireplace and hurl himself off across the room. He walked around narrow windowsills and would hide laughing behind the curtains. He didn't use the stairs for years, preferring to climb up and down the wooden spindles with both fingers and toes bent around the poles, and would walk around the very top of the banister balancing on one foot with a long open drop below. One slip or lapse of concentration could have killed him instantly, but he didn't know that and he didn't care. We would gently try to coax him down, fearing what would happen if we scared him by shouting, but nothing ever did any good, he was back up there the instant our backs were turned.

When he was younger, and he could still fit, he spent much of his time watching the TV from the top of the living room door. Again we found we couldn't deter him from this. For some reason he just felt the need to be high up and view the world from above. It became so common that we hardly noticed when he shinned up the doorframe and perched himself at the top. It was amusing though to observe other people's reactions when they visited our house. Tom made lots of friends when he started at the local primary school, so there were often parents coming and going bringing their children over to play. They would stop in fright with a startled look on their face when they realised there was a small boy sitting on top of a door or clambering around the staircase. They would recoil in horror and panic and be completely baffled at my somewhat cavalier and laid-back attitude to it all. Once they got to know Connor they understood, but at first they must have wondered if it was safe to leave their child in my care at all.

Despite having two trampolines to play on he still can't resist jumping wildly up and down on the beds and couches. For a while we put the small gym sized trampoline in his room in the vain hope of deterring him from wrecking the bed but it only seemed to make matters worse. He would take great delight in using it like an exercise circuit, bounding from the bed onto the trampoline then off that on to the floor. This routine would be repeated for literally hours without him ever getting tired or slowing down. His first bed ended up in a skip, the wooden base having been smashed to bits underneath the mattress. His wild jumping is also taking its toll on the couches too.

Luckily we have a conservatory at the back of our garden large enough to hold a twelve-foot wide trampoline. It virtually fills the room, leaving little space for anything else, but it has been a godsend. He spends loads of time playing down there and calls it his "play house". The only problem is that he prefers to play alone and gets angry when Tom tries to go in there with him, but he has to learn that it must be shared. The trampoline is probably the best thing we ever invested in and he bounces for literally hours on end while watching a film or listening to music. Of course it is completely trashed, with bent poles and ripped netting, but he loves it and needs a way of burning off some of his excess energy.

As well as the climbing and bouncing Connor likes to live his life at full speed. There is a play area near our Spanish property and he likes nothing better than to scooter around the path as fast as the wheels will carry him. He has fallen off a few times resulting in cuts, bruises and tears, but never learns the lesson of slowing down.

At a very young age he developed the ability to climb up ropes in the playground. He especially loved the bell shaped climbing frames made up of interlinked ropes with a pole up the middle. These tend to pretty high and are meant for older, more experienced climbers, but this never put him off. He would be up in seconds, swinging from one rope to the next with agility and ease, and wouldn't stop until he reached the top. Once, to our horror, he actually attempted to sit on top of the pole itself but relented when we yelled for him to stop. Visits to play areas were never happy and relaxing for us, you always had to be on your guard and could not afford to take your eyes off Connor for a second. My Mum, Dad and I would spread out and position ourselves underneath, ready to catch him if he fell. Whether we would have been successful in saving him we'll never know, but luckily he never slipped, not even once. When Tom was little he was always very wary of heights, only needing a few feet between him and the ground to send him into a cold sweat. Connor would be swinging like a monkey from rope to rope twenty feet above him, with not a care in the world.

Connors' climbing abilities extend even further, and he can often be found at the top of the old style metal lampposts we have in the back garden. He is also able to shoot up stonewalls, where there is really not much to grip on to at all. His complete lack of understanding when it comes to dangerous situations though is the scariest thing of all. I once found him sat on top of the gas hob pressing the ignition button to see what would happen. If he needs to cut paper or slice a cake he will always find the sharpest scissors or knives and attempt to do the task himself, without any thought of the possible consequences. He will stand at the edge of a road and copy the words "stop, look and listen", but he has no clue why you say them and would run out in front of a car given the chance. When we visit other peoples' houses I have to go upstairs to check that the upstairs windows are shut tight. I can't trust him not to jump out expecting to be able to fly like the super hero's he worships so much.

There was a rather worrying and embarrassing episode about four years ago on the last day of the summer term. Connor had already broken up so I had to take him with me to pick Tom up from school. As it was a lovely sunny afternoon lots of the parents decided to go to a local pub where there is a large children's outdoor play area, and as many of his friends were going Tom wanted to go too. I wasn't so keen knowing that Connor was likely to get up to some kind of mischief, but not wanting to disappoint Tom we went along regardless. We were all sitting in the garden only yards away from where the children were all playing and I was constantly checking on Connor's whereabouts. I glanced over to see him disappear round a corner of the pub building, and as he didn't immediately reappear I went to see what he was up to. There was an open gate and a staircase leading up to a flat roof above. It was only one storey, but high enough to cause major damage if you slipped and fell off. I called to Connor and he appeared at the top of the stairs, obviously angry at being found out. Reluctantly he obeyed and came down and I closed the gate as best I could, but noticed that the bolt was broken and it wouldn't shut properly. Returning to my seat I saw that Connor was back on the climbing frames and seemed to be playing happily. Distracted by another parent I took my eyes off him, but seconds later someone shouted and was pointing over to the pub. Everyone stopped to look and to my horror there was Connor running and jumping at full speed around the edge of the roof. I dived up and legging as fast as I could raced up the stairs and on to the top of the building. Hesitating for a split second I noticed that it didn't look very substantial to walk on, and there were heating pipes and flues dotted around everywhere. I yelled to Connor to come back but he was having none of it, this was far too much fun. I tentatively tiptoed around the floor half expecting it to give way at any moment. As I became more confident that it must be reasonably safe I sped up in an attempt to catch him. Seeing me coming though only made him run faster, and we ended up chasing around in circles with me screaming at the top of my voice for him to stop, and Connor ignoring me completely. There was no barrier around the edge to prevent him from going right over the side, and I was panicking that he would run right off and fall to the ground. After what seemed like an eternity, he decided to comply and slowed down enough for me to grab him. In a vice like grip I dragged him down the stairs, suddenly realising that we had been watched by dozens of families from Toms' school. Absolutely mortified I called to Tom and we left, utterly ashamed.

* * *

I never thought he could top anything he had done in the past, but he did something recently that shocked us to the core. It is probably the closest we have come to losing him, and I don't think we will ever completely get over it.

He had been playing in the conservatory on his trampoline and grazed his foot. It was nothing really, just a superficial wound and there wasn't even any blood, but as usual he was yelling

"DOCTOR!" I placed the obligatory wet piece of cold kitchen roll around it and went off to find a dressing. Not being able to find the tubular kind, I wrapped a regular long bandage round his foot and up his ankle. Satisfied that he was cured he bounded off back to the garden to resume his bouncing.

It was a nice warm evening for a change and we had decided to fire up the barbeque and cook some kebabs. While Frank went outside to clean the grill I stood by the kitchen sink cutting the chicken. A few moments later I glanced up to see Connor running towards the house with Frank close behind. Frank was yelling my name and I gathered something was seriously wrong, but nothing could have prepared me for the sight I was about to see. Having to pause to wash the raw meat of my hands, I didn't immediately realise quite what had occurred. I turned to Connor to give him my full attention and recoiled in horror. There was a thick, nasty red burn mark in a ring right around his neck. One side was worse than the other with spots of blood oozing out on to the surface of his skin. He was screaming in pain and extremely distraught, so our first thought was to treat the wound and try to calm him down. We quickly ran the cold tap and wet a tea towel. Sitting him down we carefully placed the towel around his neck so that the stinging pain could be eased by the cold. I sat and held him for at least thirty minutes until he had stopped shaking and the yelling subsided. It was only then that we could take a good look at him and figure out what had caused the accident.

Frank had looked over from the barbeque to see Connor jumping down from the trampoline; he noticed that the bandage had been tied over the top of the wooden beam that holds up the conservatory roof, and for a split second thought that he was still attached to it. We could only surmise that he had removed the bandage from his foot and thought it would be good fun to hang it over the wood and tie it around himself. Maybe he was replaying a scene from 'Scooby Doo' where the ancient mummies are wrapped in cloth from head to foot. He would have had no idea that this was dangerous or could have caused serious damage, or worse, it was just a game to him.

The doctor at the hospital assured me he was fine, and I hope that he has learnt his lesson, but Frank and I will never forget the trauma of that day.

* * *

Maybe one day, far off into the future, Connor will learn to become wary of dangerous situations, but whether he can ever master this vital lesson in life is debatable. For now, at least, we have to

98

ensure that we are always there to protect him, and to catch him if he falls.

# 7

## BAD HAIR DAYS

Never having been blessed with nice, glossy, manageable hair I often find myself in front of the bathroom mirror first thing in the morning. Even when freshly washed, my hair refuses to behave. I can prod, poke, straighten or scrunch to my heart's content but it never seems to do any good. No amount of gel can tame it either, in fact the more I pile it on, the stiffer and stickier it gets. In the end I give up and try to get through the day without catching my reflection too often. Connor seems to have inherited the 'bad hair day' gene too, but his problems are made much worse by the fact that he hates having it cut.

This isn't just a dislike for him though; this is a real, genuine fear. Even Tom still isn't overly keen on having his neck shaved but will sit and tolerate it. We then have to rush home and wash off the loose bits that are irritating his skin. Thankfully, he is still just young enough to appreciate the free lollypop you get for co-operating, but no amount of persuasion has worked up to now to get Connor into that dreaded chair. He doesn't like any kind of sweets anyway, so the promise of a tasty treat just doesn't cut it at all. Even if we could get him to sit down and have a twirl around it would be a start. I often take him along to witness Toms' hair cut, and he is quite happy to enter the shop and sit by the door, but that's as far as it goes. He can cope with quietly reading a book while waiting for his brother but that's enough. He refuses to make even one step over to the other side of the room where that scary woman is standing with her sharp scissors and noisy electric razor. You'd think her intention was to chop him up into little pieces and feed him to the lions.

We did try once, years ago, but it ended in disaster and isn't worth the amount of stress it caused him. I wrestled him into the chair but he fought me off and we ended up in a heap on the floor. As I lay on top of him tightly gripping his hands I pleaded with the hairdresser to do the best she could, and fast. She just stood there looking horrified and after a very short attempt of a few snips with the scissors, decided to give up. Connor was in a terrible state by then and I was frustrated and completely embarrassed. Tom was praying for a huge hole to appear in the floor and swallow him up. This had all been played out in front of a roomful of strangers who were all looking on in utter amazement and shock. We legged it as fast as we could, vowing never to repeat that exercise again.

Having no other choice, other than leaving it to grow long, we decided that it would have to be done at home. In the bath was the best method, as he couldn't escape easily. Jayne offered to cut it for a while until my confidence grew and I gradually took over. He still screams and shouts and twirls around in a futile attempt to evade the scissors, and I still get a fair amount of verbal insults, but on the whole it is successful. Having never been trained in the art of hair cutting it's a bit hit and miss as to how good it looks, but we really have no other option right now. As he can't stay still I often manage to cut chunks of flesh off my fingers during the process. I have considered trying to persuade a brave mobile stylist to come to the house but this would require Connor to sit still in a chair, a task he currently finds impossible. To expect a complete stranger to hover over the edge of the bath is totally unacceptable, even if I maintained Connors' dignity with a pair of swimming trunks.

At least the current situation is better than what we used to face. In the past he hated even having his hair washed let alone cut, and you were lucky if he allowed it to be brushed at all. The mere sight of the shampoo bottle would set off a massive screaming fit and he would yell abuse at me. This trauma used to shock and upset us. I felt terrible subjecting him to such terror, but he needed to be clean so it had to be done. He would scream, "DADDY, HELP ME, SHE'S AN EVIL MONSTER!" Frank would rush up the stairs totally convinced I was trying to drown him. I even got to the stage of warning anyone in the house of an impending hair cutting session so they would be prepared in advance for the noise. When no one came to his rescue he resorted to yelling to his favourite cartoon characters for help. He would shout, "SONIC, SPONGEBOB, BATMAN, HELP ME!" Really believing that they could jump out of the pages of a magazine and come to life to save him. Connor finds it very difficult to tell the difference between reality and fiction. He stared right into my eyes on one occasion and said with such venom in his voice "YOU'RE EVIL, AND THERE'S SNAKES IN THE HOUSE!"

Regardless of how stressful bath times were though, at least he would get washed. I have heard of some autistic children being that petrified of water they flatly refused to go anywhere near a bath or shower, forcing their parents to have to clean them with a wet flannel. That would be a real nightmare and I was relieved we didn't have to resort to that. As a typical little boy though, he didn't always fancy a wash, he was far too busy playing, so I often found myself chasing him round the house. Once caught you had to work fast before he got the chance of breaking free. I would lift him up and carry him to the bathroom, attempting to avoid being kicked anywhere painful. I would then have to shut us inside, guarding the door so he couldn't make his escape.

It isn't only his hair that is sacred though; anything attached to his body is deemed worthy of fighting for. Unfortunately, some things that disengage themselves naturally from the body are quickly recycled before I have the chance to intervene. Until very recently we were never allowed to cut his nails, this was strictly forbidden territory. Both finger and toenails were either picked or chewed off. I never found any strewn around the house and they didn't appear to make it to the bin either. I dread to think where they all went.

He also hasn't yet grown out of the toddler phase of devouring the contents of his nose. This, I think, is one of his most disgusting habits, which no amount of telling off by me seems to be able to stop. The worst time was when he was around three years old. He was suffering from a really bad head cold and I had gone in to nursery school early to pick him up. While I was waiting for one of the girls to retrieve his coat from the playground he had a huge sneeze and a massive dollop of snot flew out and hung on his face, stretching from his nose down to his top lip. We all screamed in unison and someone ran off to grab a box of tissues. Sadly they weren't quite fast enough and returned just in time to see the whole lot being expertly sucked in and swallowed. Connor looked so pleased with himself; after all he had cleaned up the mess hadn't he? I burst out laughing, but some of the staff turned a nice shade of green. It is hard to comprehend how he can happily consume something so vile whilst at the same time turning down so many nice foods.

We are sure that Connor has a very high pain threshold, and used to wonder if he ever felt pain at all. As he has such excellent gross motor skills he doesn't tend to get hurt much, but the odd cut is inevitable sometimes. He is tough when it comes to bumps and bruises, not seeming to notice for the most part, but if he has a cut that bleeds then the floodgates open. As a typical bloke the mere sight of blood makes him squirm, one tiny wound and he is surely dying. He rushes in from the garden screaming "DOCTOR!" I then have to wet a piece of kitchen roll and wrap it around the offending area of skin. He won't allow any antiseptic creams whatsoever, and we have long since learnt the dire consequences of going anywhere near him with a sticking plaster. Only cold water and tissue are allowed, secured with a piece of tubular bandage. Once this is in place and he can no longer see any blood the drama is over. Problem solved he happily runs off to re climb whatever it was that caused the accident in the first place. These types of bandages are great for limbs, but when Connor grazed his forehead once he just couldn't understand why I refused to put one over his face. The fact that it wouldn't actually fit, and he wouldn't be able to see or breathe through it, were completely lost on him.

One of the worst hurdles we have yet still to overcome is buying shoes. This sounds like a harmless exercise I know and is a very simple task for most families, but for children like Connor it can be an extremely scary and stressful experience. Choosing the shoes is not a problem; he is not fussy about what he wears at all. Given half a chance he would leave the house in my pink fluffy slippers if we let him. The real problem lies in the feet measuring, and having to wait his turn in the queue. He doesn't do crowds, doesn't like strangers

touching him, and the worst problem of all –
doesn't do waiting. After numerous aborted
attempts at this we have all but given up. Right now
I either guess his size by trying Tom's shoes on
him, or ring up our local branch of Mothercare who
kindly open the store early for us so that we can go
in alone. This second option has proved very
successful and we have managed a number of
stress-free shopping trips. The staff are wonderfully
understanding and extremely accommodating. They
are even happy to chase him around the store with
the foot measurer if he chooses to run off and
explore. It doesn't matter if he decides to lie on the
floor, do monkey impressions, or clamber around
the furniture. There is no one there to point or stare
or comment on his behaviour. You may think this
sounds ridiculous, having to go to such elaborate
lengths just to get his shoe size, but if you'd
witnessed some of our previous outings you'd
understand the difficulties involved.

The worst episode we had was about three years
ago. The boys and I had driven over to my parents'
house so they could come with us for moral support.
We were confident that if there were enough of us
we would be able to control him, no problem. We
drove to a shopping complex about ten minutes
away. As it was the school holidays it was heaving

with shoppers. This was really not an ideal time to go with Connor but they were due back to school in a few days and really needed new shoes. I managed to park close to where we were going but as we headed for the door he scanned the other shops and spotted a large DVD store across the car park. That proved to be fatal, and was, I guess, the cause of the horrendous tantrum that was to follow.

I fought my way through the crowds and retrieved a numbered ticket from the machine. There were at least fifteen to twenty people in front of us, and we knew we were in for a lengthy wait. Having no-where to sit down we split ourselves up and hovered around the store monitoring Connors' movements. After a few minutes exploring he was quickly bored and decided to make a break for it. Unfortunately for my Dad he just happened to be closest to the front entrance so he made a grab for Connor as he tried to scoot past. Desperate to escape he decided to let loose one of his loudest screaming fits to date. My poor Dad looked totally shocked as he held on for dear life. He had never seen one of Connors' worst tantrums before and felt, I think, rather out of his depth. I made my way forward from the back of the room, pushing past some people and climbing over others in an attempt to get there as fast as I could. Connor is very agile and has the ability to wriggle out of the strongest of grips in seconds. I didn't rate my Dads' chances of keeping control of him very highly at all. By now my Mum had reached them too and we all tried to calm him down but it was no use. Once he has set his mind on something nothing in the world can change it. He was determined to escape the mayhem and go off in search of DVDs; we were determined to keep him in the shoe shop. There was only going to be one winner in this fight and I guessed it probably wouldn't be us. He was now writhing around the floor yelling, while my Dad and I blocked the way out. The sound levels were through the roof, they must have been able to hear him three stores down. He was screaming and kicking, with tears rolling down his cheeks and the anger clear in his eyes. It was like he was fighting for his very life he was so distraught. I had recounted these visits to my Mum and Dad before but nothing could have prepared them for this outburst. Even I was surprised at the severity of it all, and Tom had long since disappeared off to the back of the store in an attempt to pretend he wasn't actually with us. I suppose, in hindsight, we should have let him either go and choose a DVD first, or abandoned the visit and tried again later, but I had little conviction that he would entertain the idea of coming back. With school only days away it was essential that we stuck it out for as long as possible. After a good twenty to thirty minutes of causing complete havoc he showed no signs of giving up. Everyone was staring at us, amazed at this circus going on right in front of them. I felt destroyed and was fighting back the tears, not wishing to embarrass myself any further. At long last one of the staff used some initiative and led us over to one corner where it was quieter. Even though it was still not our turn she took pity on us, and offered to use the portable hand held device to measure his feet, as there was obviously no way on earth he was going to stand still on the electronic scale. I just nodded in relief, not trusting myself to try and speak. I knew the floodgates would open if I uttered one word to anyone. With all three of us on top of him we managed to keep him still long enough for a reading to be taken. This over, my Mum and Dad took him outside while I waited for a printout of his size. I would take this to another store closer to home and buy the shoes another time; the opportunity of trying any on had well and truly passed for that day. Piece of paper in hand, I stepped outside to join my parents. I felt completely drained and frustrated. Trying to appreciate it from Connors' point of view, but so saddened that we couldn't just blend in with all the other families out that afternoon. Once out in the open he was happy again. The outburst forgotten, he happily toddled off in the direction of the DVD shop with us all jogging behind. He had no clue what he had just put us through, and didn't give a toss. Years later I think we are all still traumatised by that trip.

# 8

## SUPERMARKET DASH

Visiting a supermarket with young children on a busy Saturday afternoon is not a nice prospect for any parent. The aisles are packed with people double parking their trolleys; stopping to have a chat with a friend they've just bumped into. There are youngsters repeatedly pestering their mums and dads to buy them something they've already been told they can't have. The staff always feel the need to fill up the shelves at the worst possible times, blocking the way with the large metal cages used to transport the goods. It can be a stressful, daunting and exhausting experience, resulting in some very bad tempered parents and tearful children by the end of the trip.

Envisage your worst nightmare where your child runs off round a corner and disappears into the crowd. Gone in seconds, and in your panic you can't even recall what colour clothes they were wearing. Imagine the worst screaming fit your child could muster, so loud that the whole store can hear it, and everyone stops to look. Imagine having to physically restrain them and drag them out of the shop, kicking and screaming, then they fight their way free and end up nearly under the wheels of a car. Imagine this scenario then times it by a factor of 100. Now you have an idea of what a trip out to a supermarket on a busy Saturday afternoon can be like with a child who has autism.

I have lost count of the number of horrendous shopping trips I have had with Connor. There have been so many that they all start to merge together in the memory banks after a while. They are made much worse when the stores are busy, but we have had some equally unpleasant encounters at quieter periods too. It often depends on a number of factors as to how bad it might be. He could be in a mood that day or expected to be going somewhere else. The worst thing is you have no idea what will happen until you get there, and by then it is much too late. There are no warning signs of an impending tantrum, and no defence mechanisms you can put into place to prevent it. You have to just take the risk and go, and be prepared to suffer the consequences. I used to get really upset when he misbehaved during a shopping trip and it would take me hours to wind down when we got home. I got to the point of avoiding taking him out as much as possible, even paying a babysitter to watch him while I nipped out to buy a pint of milk. I couldn't handle the stress it caused, but this was no good as a long-term solution. He was never going to learn how to behave in public if he was never allowed out of the house.

Going out anywhere with an autistic child can be very challenging, but supermarkets especially seem to be particularly bad. Maybe there are just too many stimulants in the environment for them to cope with all at once. They all tend to be very big and bright with white shiny floors, and extremely noisy and busy. Even the strip lights that hang down from the roof give off a buzzing sound that most of us wouldn't really notice, but to a child with heightened senses something that appears relatively mild to us can cause a complete system overload.

When Connor was younger he seemed to really struggle with all aspects of these stores. Whilst he was still small enough to fit into the seat in the shopping trolley things were bearable. You could never get past the magazine rack by the front entrance without having to choose at least three or four, but once he was satisfied I was able to carry on without too much bother. He would sit happily thumbing through the pages whilst I dashed up and down the aisles, only having a limited amount of time to grab the essentials we really needed. You weren't able to saunter along slowly, take the time to read a label, or pause to compare two similar items to ensure you were getting the best value for money. There was to be none of that. I even had to avoid anyone I knew in case they wanted to stop for a chat, and there was no time to waste in the bread-slicing queue or at the fresh fish counter. It was a case of grab and go, before he got to the end of the last magazine, passing through the checkout had to be factored into this short time window too. But at least it was manageable, and meant that I could shop reasonably stress free. It was when he grew bigger then the real fun began.

I had put this day off for as long as was humanly possible, predicting just how bad it would be when he was free to roam. Even when he was really far too large and heavy to be in the trolley, I would still struggle to lift him up and squeeze him in, desperate to delay the inevitable for as long as I could. If getting him in was difficult enough then extracting him was even worse, I would pull and heave as he struggled to free his trapped legs. Eventually though, I had to concede defeat. I was worried that he would get hurt, or that his weight would tip up the trolley. I had always dreaded what he would do when allowed to run wild but some of his behaviour surpassed even my worst expectations.

He escaped at every opportunity, and as he was so fast could disappear in an instant. He wasn't trying to be naughty, just wanted to go and find the items that he liked, but it was exhausting having to constantly rush round at full speed to find out where he'd gone. I never knew if he intended to come back, or if he would be able to find me. I always worried that he would run out into the car park if he couldn't locate me in the store, and as has he has no road sense at all, would end up seriously hurt or worse. He had no interest in helping me choose the things I needed, no desire to stay close by or hold my hand, and no patience whatsoever to visit each aisle in turn so that we didn't miss anything. I didn't dare try to use the distraction of letting him push the trolley for fear of whom or what he might crash in to. He rarely looks where he is going and nobody wants the back of their heels crushed by an out of control maniac. I quickly discovered that it was safer to allow him to choose his favourite things first then make an attempt to get whatever else I wanted. You had to be reasonably fast, he wasn't prepared to hang around for long, but at least it meant I could take him with me when there was no one home to look after him.

The main problem we have now is trying to limit what he is allowed to buy during each shopping trip. He used to fly into a terrible tantrum if he couldn't get his own way; there was murder if I said no to anything he wanted. He would lie down on the floor, literally kicking, screaming and banging his clenched fists on the hard floor. He would yell at the top of his voice, so loud that people would stop and stare at him. I would gently try to peel him off the ground, pretending that I wasn't the least bit phased by his behaviour. I would attempt to appear calm and collected, while inside I was cringing, tears of frustration very close to pouring out. I always seemed to manage to make it home before breaking down, determined not to cause myself any more embarrassment. I happened to bump into the father of a child from Tom's school one day. As luck would have it Connor was lying on the floor in the toy aisle, meowing very loudly like a cat, as the dad turned the corner. Standing with Connor between us we casually exchanged pleasantries, as you do with people you don't know that well, how are you today, comments about the weather etc. Meanwhile, my child was happily imitating animal sounds, with arms and legs spread wide on the floor. Smiling and nodding I had to make it seem that this was completely normal behaviour in the middle of a busy supermarket.

He still insists on running off in search of his favourite items, but at least now I have managed to cut down the number of things he is allowed and he accepts this without too much of a tantrum. He can now choose two or three magazines instead of wanting six and one DVD as opposed to three or four. We can negotiate in the toy aisle and make him choose something small in place of an expensive one. He always wants to get his favourite cereals, pretzels, crackers, donuts and ice cream but that's fine as he only picks those he likes so nothing is wasted. It is a good lesson for him to learn to have to choose between two things that he wants. The fact that he can do this now without a massive fight is good progress and a huge improvement on the past, not to mention a blessing on the cash flow front.

Queuing at the checkout has also improved significantly. Waiting for anything has always been very hard for Connor, as I don't think he really understood quite what he was waiting for. He would lie down in protest and yell at the top of his voice. I could feel the eyes of the other customers burning into my back as I unpacked the trolley at breakneck speed whilst smiling at the checkout assistant pretending that nothing was wrong. I lost count of the number of times I had to rush off down the shop and drag him back kicking and screaming, jamming him in between me and the counter while at the same time attempting to pack the bags as fast as possible. He also didn't know why he needed to hand over his purchases to be scanned at the till. He would cling on to them for dear life and I would have to go into a long explanation as to why this was such a problem for him. I would warn the member of staff that when I managed to prise an item off him it would immediately trigger a huge screaming fit. They would have to scan it as quickly as possible and hand it back to put a halt to the yelling. Some people looked at me in total confusion, and I think disbelief, until they actually witnessed what happened the second I removed the prized possession out of Connors hands. Once the beloved object was safely back in his grip the tantrum would subside as quickly as it had begun and was forgotten in an instant by him. I though, took a lot longer to recover from each bout of yelling and would store them up in the 'bad trips out' file in my head, each one chipping away at my resolve, my strength, and my very soul.

Luckily these days, things are so much better. We are still unable to visit anywhere without him getting something but at least he is open to a little negotiation now. He no longer fights me at the checkout and will even help unpack the trolley, handing the goods to me to place on the belt. I think he is happier to be involved in the whole process, and feels some sense of achievement and self worth. Once everything is safely laid out he says "good teamwork Mummy", I still have to pack the bags myself but that is probably a blessing.

We recently went through a phase of having to get passport photos each time we went anywhere there was an instant photo booth. He would rush over and sit in them, flatly refusing to come out until his picture was taken. He has now realised that your face needs to be in the circle on the screen for it to work properly and avoid missing off half your head, but at first this didn't register at all. I have a great collection of photos now, most with nice big grins on them. Ironically, when I actually needed to renew his passport a few years ago he refused to cooperate at all. After various attempts resulting in some terrible and unusable pictures we took him to a store where you stand in front of a plain background and the image is taken with a digital camera. At least this way you can keep going until the desired result is achieved, at no extra cost. Of course he behaved like an angel and we got a suitable photo first time round.

One thing he still loves to do is stroke peoples' skin. He just wants to feel the texture and seems fascinated, especially with girls' arms. Thankfully he hasn't attempted to touch up any men yet! Around the ages of four to six he would often go up to someone in a shop and stroke up and down their arms. Initially this shocked people, especially if they had their back to us, but most were fine about it when they turned around and saw him. Not having the strength to go into a big explanation every time, I usually just apologised and quickly pulled him away. There was however one really embarrassing situation one day at our local branch of Tesco's, where one unsuspecting poor woman got rather more than she bargained for. As we entered the store he broke free from my grip and headed towards the rows of magazines situated just inside the entrance. Right next to the kids section is a separate area housing the daily newspapers where the shopper happened to be leaning over, engrossed in reading one of the articles. As Connor rushed past he obviously took a liking to this lady. Seizing his opportunity he paused for a split second, enjoyed a brief grope of her backside, and then continued on his way. Being a few paces behind I glanced over just in time to realise what had happened and I froze in horror. The woman turned round, frantically scanning the immediate vicinity for the pervert who had dared to squeeze her bottom. She hadn't realised it was Connor, as he had moved so fast that he had gone before she even turned around. I was faced with a split second decision; go over and apologise or walk away, pretending I hadn't witnessed the incident. Of course I had to do the right thing and put her mind at rest. I went over and explained about his autism. As he was only six she was fine about it, and I think rather relieved that it hadn't been an old man in a raincoat and slippers. I walked away, my cheeks red from shame and embarrassment.

I pray to God that one day he'll grow out of this or learn to accept that grabbing strangers in the street is an unacceptable form of behaviour. You can just about get away with it when you are six and cute, but as a strapping sixteen year old lad you'll either receive a slap across the face or a prison sentence. Hopefully this message will sink in sooner rather than later.

I really thought he was making good progress in the 'how to behave in the supermarket' area, but we had a setback quite recently that took me by surprise. I was alone with Connor in a Sainsbury's store a few miles from home. He seemed calm that day and I had high hopes of a stress free outing for once, when suddenly he turned on me and started yelling. Not immediately seeing what had caused this outburst I tried to hush him and carry on. By then we were over half way round and I didn't want to have to abandon the shopping and walk out. I kept going with one hand pushing the trolley and the other gripped around Connors' wrist. He was terribly agitated, desperately fighting me with his hands and crying loudly. He started shouting "GET ME OUT OF HERE" at the top of his voice, and people were starting to stop and stare at us. We battled on and he appeared to be relaxing a little when a couple with a child, about a year younger than Connor, turned into our aisle. Coming face to face with them Connor freaked out. He managed to escape my hold on him and legged off round the nearest corner as fast as he could. Quite shocked at this sudden outburst I chased after him, eventually cornering him in the next section. As verbal communication is still difficult for Connor, he had no way of explaining what was wrong. I wanted him to shut up as by now the whole store was watching and I was becoming increasingly self-conscious. Determined to grab the last few things we needed I rushed him along, but each time we turned a corner the couple with the little boy were there and Connor was distraught. It was then that I realised what was the cause of his tantrum. The child was happily sitting in their trolley, emitting a fairly low, but repetitive, kind of grunt. He was doing this constantly and I guessed that he also possibly suffered from problems similar to Connors' own. The noise was that quiet that I hadn't noticed at first, but Connor must have picked up on it instantly and he couldn't stand listening to it. Deciding we needed to get out fast, I headed towards the checkout. It was a fight to stop him from running off and pack the shopping at the same time. I held him tightly between my legs as he lay on the floor yelling with his hands over his ears. As I waited to pay, the couple appeared at the next till and were staring at us along with everyone else. I had half hoped they might realise what was causing Connors' outburst and stay away from us, but it didn't seem so. Having paid at last we escaped the store and I literally fell out the door in relief. The tantrum subsided as rapidly as it had started and I drove home in a state of shock and sadness. Yet again I had had to endure a very stressful trip. Yet again not one person had shown any compassion, or offered the slightest bit of help.

# 9

## DELICIOUS TOMATOES

Many children perceive healthy food as being totally vile and gross. When confronted by a sprout or a stick of celery they would rather go and flush their head down the toilet than take even the smallest of nibbles. If presented with a lovely freshly baked wholemeal bun or a large juicy pear the reaction is often the same. Although, I have to agree on the sprout situation, they must be the worst vegetable you could ever imagine having to swallow. I recall my mum attempting to get us to eat at least one during every Christmas dinner when we were growing up. I'm sure it did us no harm, but I never did grow to like them at all. I do love lots of fruits and vegetables and always encourage Tom to at least try a taste of things, to see if he likes them. But I would never force-feed him something that I wasn't prepared to eat myself. Even the dog will snack on a raw carrot, but prefers a nice tasty sausage, given half a chance.

Due to Franks' work commitments it is virtually impossible to live a nine to five type of life in our house. He is away a lot of the time, and when he is home has to work most nights, resulting in some very late dinners more often than not. Obviously the children can't eat at this time, so end up having their food separately from us. This arrangement is not conducive to good family relations I know. It is well documented that this is an ideal time for everyone to get together, eat a nice leisurely meal, and chat about the days' events. This kind of cosy, happy vision is completely alien to us. The fact that Connor won't sit still for more than a couple of seconds and is incapable of 'chatting' doesn't do much to help.

* * *

If your child requested 'delicious tomatoes' for their breakfast you'd be delighted that you had done such a good job as a parent. All your persistent efforts to educate them in the wonderful world of healthy eating were finally paying off. You would surely feel so proud, and give yourself a well-deserved pat on the back. When Connor asks for this for his breakfast though, it isn't what he actually means. If I presented him with a nice plate of either cooked or cold tomatoes, he would look at me with utter contempt. Would push the plate back

126

at me; horrified that I would dare to subject him to such a dreadful and disgusting sight. He would scream a loud "YUCK", hold his nose, and yell defiantly "NO, STINKY". He would run off, arms flailing in the air, waving madly like a wild banshee. Unfortunately, this is his reaction to lots of foods, most in fact. Anything that is not boring, salty, hard, crunchy, bland, sugary or able to be eaten with your fingers is deemed completely inedible. He refuses to even smell foods, let alone taste them. Whenever I am preparing anything from baked potatoes or a simple ham sandwich, to spicy Cajun chicken or a hot curry, I put it in front of Connors' nose for a reaction. I always know beforehand what this reaction will be, and it is always the same, but I live in hope, that maybe one-day, way into the future, he might attempt to try something different. At school they often cook basic recipes with the children, I think both to teach them to cook and learn about new foods. In his school bag lives a notebook that they write in and we can respond whenever we wish. Some days neither party writes at all, but as Connor cannot tell me about any aspect of his day it is a vital link between the teachers and his home life. They wrote one day recently, inquiring as to which toppings he would fancy on a pizza as they were cooking them later that week. I had to laugh, and wrote in the book 'it won't matter what you put on it, he would never, never eat it anyway'. Of course I was right, they all had a lovely time preparing the food and Connor joined in enthusiastically. When they were ready for consumption he gave a loud "YUCK" and showed complete distaste. You'd think he had been offered a bowl of live wriggling worms or raw fish heads instead, both actually being classed as quite a delicacy in some parts of the world.

* * *

It is difficult to comprehend how Connor survives on the small amount he consumes. He is pretty skinny, but adversely extremely fit and athletic. His whole body is muscle there is no amount of fat there at all. It appears he lives on fresh air alone, eating very little or virtually nothing most days. Amazingly he had boundless energy, but we have no idea where he gets it from. I often wonder that if he did eat more would his energy levels go through the roof? He must be consuming enough to get by, but not having a varied or healthy diet can't possibly be good for him. We really don't know what else to do though. We can't physically force him to eat anything he doesn't want to, and to make mealtimes a battlefield will only cause more heartache. It just isn't worth the distress it would cause. I swear that Connor would starve himself to death rather than eat something he didn't like. I am sure he doesn't appreciate the importance of eating, or understand how much his body needs essential nutrients to function properly. He has no clue that food is his source of energy and that his brain feeds directly off what he puts in his mouth. We even used to wonder if he ever really felt hunger, but these days he will actually say he is hungry, whilst holding up his top and pointing to his stomach to show me where the food goes. He needs to learn that meals are meant to be savoured and enjoyed, not just gulped down in seconds so you can rush off and play. He is far too busy to waste precious time sitting still; even when he does eat it is done reluctantly. Most things are consumed whilst on the move; he has long since mastered the art of eating at the same time as running, jumping or climbing. I have even caught him eating whilst upside down watching TV. The only one meal he will sit for is breakfast when he wants milk on his cereal. Thankfully, he will actually finish this before darting back up again. Food appears to be a non-essential annoyance in Connors' opinion.

* * *

At least now he is capable of telling us what he fancies. We suffered years of him just standing in the middle of the kitchen pointing and screaming, with us frantically searching the cupboards, desperate to find what it was that he wanted. Now I can list exactly what he will or won't eat but back then, things were different. Each time you showed him a food he didn't like the hysterics would get louder. It was a race against time to discover the right item before total mayhem set in. This scenario went on day after day, year after long year, and was extremely wearing for us all. He now has a very limited list of things he is willing to consume. Most of them are hard, plain, or high in salt like crackers, cereals, biscuits, toast, and his all time favourite – pretzels. The only soft food he tends to go for is cake. He will eat chips if they have salt on, preferring the thin skinny ones to the chunky type. He would quite happily live at McDonalds if we let him; he loves their fries so much. If we get chips from the Chinese takeaway he prods around to find the hard, crunchy ones, which sit at the bottom of the packet. The ones which have been repeatedly cooked, and would normally be rejected and thrown away by most people. We are tempted to go and ask them to delve deep in to the depths of their chip pans and make him a whole packet of these leftover morsels. That would be chip heaven to Connor.

Up to about four years ago, he would eat both fish fingers and chicken nuggets. The fish had to be Birds Eye, with a coating of breadcrumbs, never batter. He would even check out the packaging to make sure I was not trying to fool him. Fat chance of that anyway, as he can detect even the tiniest of changes in both smell and taste. He would be an excellent candidate, when he grows older, for those game shows where you are blindfolded and have to identify items by only touch or smell. The only nuggets he would ever eat were from McDonalds. He would never touch ones I cooked at home. I tried all the varieties I could find, always checking the ingredients to ensure that only chicken breast meat was used. I even bought breadcrumbs and made them myself, but all these efforts were wasted. Not one bite of chicken was going to pass his lips if it wasn't from his favourite fast food outlet. Seemingly though, virtually overnight, he suddenly took a dislike to both of these foods and has never touched a fish finger or a nugget again. We are completely baffled as to why this happened. Possibly the recipes have been slightly altered in some way, undetectable to most palates, but very significant to Connor. Maybe nothing was changed at all; he just made the decision that he didn't like them anymore. Very strange though, that he went off both things at around the same time. I have read that this can be quite common in people with Autism. That they will eat a certain thing for years then suddenly stop, and more often than not, never eat it again. This would appear to be totally insane behaviour to the rest of us, but there must be some logical reason why they do it. So much more research needs to be done in order to help those with this condition. Connor has now cut off his main source of protein, and try as we may, he seems determined to stay this way. We would really love some guidance over how to tackle his eating habits, as we have run out of ideas. I have considered trying to blackmail him, use something he really wants to make him consume a food he currently refuses. I could wave his McDonalds chips in his face in an attempt to make him maybe just lick a slice of apple, but I am worried that if we turn eating into a fight then he will stop altogether.

Even the foods he will eat come with certain stipulations and strict rules. If he fancies a cracker it can't be just any old thing. Supermarket own brands, or flavoured types, get thrown in disgust. They must always be 'Jacobs' cream crackers in an orange and white packet. You can't deceive him as he knows exactly what they look like, and even the precise location of them in all the shops we visit.

They have to be whole, broken ones don't taste the same, and they need a decent coating of margarine, strictly not butter. Given the chance he will spread this on himself but tends to be a little too generous for my liking. I end up having to scrape off the excess two inches back in to the tub while he looks on in annoyance. He will also scoop up a finger full and try to eat it before I have the chance to stop him. Whenever he puts on his Wallace and Gromit DVD's we have to rush into the kitchen to make crackers as Wallace loves to eat them.

Thankfully, when it comes to cereals he is quite flexible. There must be at least four different types he will happily consume either with or without milk. Over time we have successfully weaned him off the need for sugar, although he still insists on having a small amount on Weetabix. Can't really blame him for that one, they are quite boring otherwise. Amazingly he loves bran flakes, usually dry. I too enjoy these with milk, but on their own it's more like chewing tough bits of cardboard, very healthy for you though. He does tend to steer towards the sugar coated varieties which are obviously not good for the teeth at all, more so in his case as teeth brushing is such an issue, but we cave in and let him have them. The cereal manufacturers must spend thousands on research in to how to entice children with irresistible flavours and textures and exciting advertising campaigns featuring the latest favourite TV character. They must rub their hands with glee as their products fly off the shelves, not caring one jot about the oral health of the child.

He will eat some biscuits, but again certain protocol prevails. Custard creams tend to be favourite; closely followed by the chocolate variety, namely bourbons. He has been known to down a shortbread or two, preferring the plainer ones than those with extra sugar on top, and even a malted milk has passed his lips on the odd occasion. He also loves to cook his own biscuits, choosing the boxed ready-made packet mixes from the supermarket. They always have cartoon characters on the front with a matching plastic shaper to mould the biscuits. I make him read the instructions on the back and he really enjoys stirring the mixture and rolling out the dough. If you don't get them in the oven fast enough, half of it gets eaten raw. When they are cooked they tend to taste awfully bland to me, but he seems to like that.

Pretzels are a huge favourite, only the hard salty type; never the soft doughy variety served warm, American style. He also only likes certain makes and specific shapes too. At home in the UK there are only two he prefers, the 'Penn State' or Sainsbury's' own brand. These are the small round twisted shaped ones. I once made the mistake of buying the large Penn State ones, exactly the same, only marginally bigger. They were immediately rejected with a resounding "YUCK" and I was put in my place for making such a dreadful mistake. On holiday in Spain he goes for the long stick like ones, again only certain makes will suffice. He has named them 'finger pretzels', and waggles his fingers around in the air to get his point across.

We also tend to buy French sticks each day when we are away in Spain and he will eat slices of this dry, with no spread or topping whatsoever. If we told people that we fed our child plain chunks of bread for his lunch they would surely class us as being cruel and nasty parents. I have in the past, discovered our loaves sat on the kitchen worktop with both ends neatly chewed off.

Cakes are also a big favourite of Connors. Small plain fairy cakes with no icing, preferably those we make at home rather than shop bought ones. We allow him the odd donut every now and then, but as these are so sugary and bad for the teeth I limit these to an occasional treat. Luckily he only likes one certain type and more often than not the shops have run out of them, which is a good thing. He scours the shelves, hunting out his favourite. They have to be ring shaped with pink icing on the top, nothing else will do. Once he is satisfied that there aren't any there he is happy to walk away empty handed. He will eat chocolate cakes as well, but again only certain ones. Right now he favours a large rectangular shaped Cadbury buttons one, which is quite plain with no cream in the middle. The nice tasty buttons get lashed aside and he eats the sponge on its own. We have to hide it as he will eat the whole cake in one go given half a chance.

As well as cooking biscuits at home Connor loves to choose readymade cake mixtures that also come in a box. These are very easy for him to make as you only have to add an egg and a few spoons of milk, so he feels he has made them all by himself. One morning, during a half term holiday, he had got up around 6am and gone downstairs. I heard him make himself a drink and turn on the TV. Assuming he was now settled and had everything he needed, I decided to stay in bed for a bit longer. About half an hour later I was woken by loud banging noises coming from the kitchen. Reluctantly, I decided I'd better go and see what it was so I slowly dragged myself out of bed and down the stairs, taking a moment to visit the bathroom on the way. The sight in the kitchen made me stop dead. Connor had, by now, happily wandered back to play in the living room, apparently oblivious to the devastation left behind. He must have been feeling rather peckish, and as I wasn't there to help, had made the decision to cook some fairy cakes on his own. Luckily he hadn't attempted to turn on the cooker, but he had made the cake mixture. Sadly, not being able to read the instructions on the box without my help, he had made up his own recipe. Instead of adding a few spoons of milk it looked like a whole pint had gone in. He had then correctly added the mix of flour and sugar and remembered the need to put in an egg. Not really grasping the concept of removing the egg from its shell first, the whole lot had gone in. Not content with just dropping the egg in whole, he had smashed it to pieces with the rolling pin first, then scooped it up as best he could off the worktop with his bare hands. Hence the noise that woke me up. The result, as you can imagine, was an absolute nightmare. There was milk and egg smeared all over the worktops, pouring down the cupboard doors, and forming puddles on the floor. It was also obvious that he had paddled in it too. The paper cake cases had been spread out on a tray and were overflowing with the mixture, whilst the bits of crushed eggshell floated on top. I just stood there in total shock, not quite sure where to start. It served me right for trying to have a lie in for once, must remember not to do that again. His only redeeming factor was that he had made an attempt to clear up the mess. There were soggy lumps of kitchen roll dotted around the place, and most importantly, he had put on an apron.

* * *

The only other thing Connor will eat is vanilla ice cream, preferably in a cone. The school cook says they try to tempt him with other foods at lunchtime but in the end give in and make him toast. I have had reports that on the odd occasion he has tried some potato waffle, sponge and custard and a baked bean or two. He refuses all these foods when we offer them at home.

It sounds like we are being too soft, pandering to his desires instead of instilling some boundaries and gaining control. But if you know anything about autism you will understand the issues we are facing. All we can do is keep on trying, in the hope that one day he will change his habits and try something new. There are only two drinks he will go near as well. He loves banana-flavoured milkshake, but won't entertain milk on its own, and he chain drinks blackcurrant juice throughout the day. Sometimes I find him with two cups at the same time, and he insists on taking a drink to bed. But again only certain brands and specific tastes will do. Luckily, he likes the no added sugar types, so that's a start. This becomes a nuisance when, on the rare occasions we are brave enough to venture out of the house, we can't find a drink that he likes. We have to always try to remember to take his juice and cup with us.

* * *

So, when Connor requests 'delicious tomatoes' for his breakfast we don't jump up and down in delight. We know he doesn't actually want tomatoes. What he really means is jam on toast. Not any old bread though, only a very few specific varieties are accepted. He has to have butter, margarine is strictly for use on crackers only, and the jam can be only one type. Strawberry flavour, with no bits in. The toast must be either cut into triangles or left whole with an imprint of SpongeBob, Scooby Doo, or Thomas the Tank Engine on it. This strict protocol must be adhered to at all times. No exceptions. No alternatives. No changes, whatsoever.

# 10

## VENTURING OUT

It can often be stressful for any parent when taking their children out for the day, but with so many places to choose from it is tempting to just throw together a picnic, pack up the car, and head off to the nearest park or drive to the coast to find a nice beach. There are forests to explore, child friendly farms to visit, beautiful country parks to walk in, and you can always find a duck of two grateful for a slice of stale bread. Even the prospect of traffic jams, travel sickness, and long journeys in a hot car with no air conditioning, doesn't put most people off. Overcrowded beaches, melted chocolate bars, sand covered sandwiches and cheeky seagulls still aren't enough to deter us, and it is well worth being drenched by an unexpected rainstorm to get out of the house for a while. Inevitably the kids may end up cranky and bored, and you arrive back home exhausted and relieved, yet happy in the knowledge that a great time was had, by all.

For the parents of an autistic child though, this scenario may be very far removed from their actual reality. Any trip away from home, however small and seemingly insignificant, can be a potential nightmare. This is where we have found we have the most trouble with Connor. He has always been difficult to control at home, but when let out to run free the gloves are off.

All our lives revolve around Connor. Everything we do and everywhere we go has to be carefully planned and orchestrated to suit his specific needs and behaviours. Carefree family vacations are an impossibility for us, and there is no such thing as a 'quick pop to the shops for a newspaper or a pint of milk'. Every single outing, whether it be for five minutes, five hours, or five days, has to be planned with military style precision down to the minutest of details. Each separate aspect has to be carefully considered, from what he will wear and what he needs to take with him, to how he will react when we get there and how far away we will have to park. Even the route itself has to be factored in, as passing certain places have been known to cause some long and very audible tantrums in the past. I have learnt the hard way after enduring many unbelievable yelling fits in the car over the years. I know this all sounds rather ridiculous and way over the top, but if you'd witnessed some of our journeys with Connor, believe me you'd understand. If asked to rate them on a stress scale of 1 to 10, then most would score the full 10 or more.

\* \* \*

I paid the price of my stupidity once when I dared to visit the local Chinese take-away when Frank was travelling. I never used to go when he was away, as having no one to watch the boys; I had to take them with me. The shop is literally less than two minutes drive from our house and we don't even pass anywhere on the way that would trigger a tantrum, but Connor had other ideas. It was a Friday night and Tom and I decided to get a nice meal and then eat it whilst watching a favourite movie. Connor was well behaved at first, and he waited patiently for the food to be cooked. He happily got back in the car but when I pulled up the path all hell broke loose. He repeatedly screamed "TOYS R US" at the top of his voice and refused to get out of the car. He had obviously thought that was where we were going, despite the fact that it was night time, and the store was actually closed. Determined to get his own way, he wedged himself half under the front passenger seat, and wouldn't budge. Equally determined to get my dinner before it was cold, and knowing I couldn't leave him there to calm down, I dragged him out and carried him into the house. Laying him down in the hall I walked away, but seconds later, I heard the front door open and was just in time to see Connor running off in to the darkness. Catching up with him at the gate he was again marched back inside; I locked the door and hid the keys in my pocket. By now he was livid, and locking him in did nothing to quell his anger. He stood in the hall banging hard on the door with his clenched fists, crying and screaming at the top of his voice. I attempted to reason with him and promised a trip to the toy shop the next day, but he was way past listening to anything I had to say. He wanted to go right now, there and then, nothing else would do. Giving up, Tom and I left him to it and settled down to watch our movie in peace, having to close the living room door to muffle the yells. I had thought that after half an hour or so he would give up, too tired to cry anymore if nothing else, but I was wrong. He banged and thumped the front door for four long hours, the walls and hall radiator became targets too. The frustration was immense, and he was red in the face from the tears and pure anger. He periodically burst into the room and forced his hands into my jeans pocket in an attempt to retrieve the keys; I had never seen him so desperate to escape. Without saying a word, it only made matters worse; I silently carried him upstairs and left him on his bed, sobbing into the pillow. Each time he came down I took him back up; he needed to be alone to calm down. Trying to make the best of things, Tom and I continued to watch our film, not actually hearing a word of it over the deafening noise. Even for my favourite chicken fried rice, I decided it just wasn't worth the grief it had caused.

* * *

Up to the age of around six and a half we had terrible trouble going anywhere. If you dared to drive past a play area or fast food outlet without stopping, there was murder. Trying to distract him in the car, so he didn't look out of the window, very rarely worked as he quickly learnt the way to all his favourite places. Even the forty- minute drive to my parents' house became a nightmare for a long while, and still is on a bad day. My usual route would mean us passing at least three places that would trigger a tantrum if I didn't stop at them. Not wanting the forty minutes to stretch into a three-hour journey I resorted to driving different ways in an attempt to avoid certain roads. It would add miles onto our trip but was preferable to a high pitched screaming fit. This strategy, although a bit of a nuisance, did work for a while, but I couldn't avoid the mile and a half long tunnel we needed to go through to get across the river. He used to yell the whole way through, then stop the instant we emerged on the other side. This ritual went on for years, each time we drove through it, and was quite a distraction when you are trying to concentrate. Connor would be screaming "LET ME OUT", punching the window, with tears pouring down his face. Tom would attempt to speak over the din, asking questions like "what will happen if the roof splits open and all the water gets in?" and "what do we do if the car goes on fire?" Not wanting to lie, or tell the truth and scare him, I often pretended I couldn't hear above all the noise. It was a relief to make it through the tunnel with my nerves still intact.

We got to the stage of having to do everything apart. Trying to go out as a whole family proved just too difficult. It was easier for either Frank or I to go out alone and leave the other one behind to look after the boys. This arrangement did nothing to help our own relationship and wasn't really healthy for any of us, but we couldn't face the unpredictability that Connor brought to what should be a simple trip out of the house. School holidays were always the worst times for me as I felt completely locked in, imprisoned in our own home, albeit by my own choice. I became scared to go anywhere, but it wasn't fair on Tom as he was missing out on so much.

When he was younger, Connor understood very little of what was said to him, and he was incapable of expressing his needs and desires to us. Standing at the front door yelling and trying to break it down with his bare fists was a big clue that he was fed up and wanted to go out, as was taking every opportunity to escape and run off down the path with me in hot pursuit. I was reasonably confident that the back garden was secure, but we live on a busy main road with cars, buses and lorries thundering past at forty miles an hour. Even an adult wouldn't stand much chance of survival, but for a small child with no road sense whatsoever, it was a suicide mission. I still have to keep the front door locked when it's just me and the boys at home, not daring to take a shower without turning the key first. I still don't trust him not to wander off or open the door to a stranger. It doesn't matter to Connor that he doesn't recognise a visitor, his brain tells him to open the door each time the bell rings, regardless of who is there. Anyone would be welcomed in, from a Nun with a box of fluffy bunny rabbits, to a ten-foot tall axe-wielding murderer. Connor is not prejudiced or biased in any way, treating everyone as an equal regardless of looks, size, age, colour, race, religion, beliefs or disability. He does however have a problem with facemasks; he still seems unable to recognise that it is just a human in a costume.

We happened to visit our local Tesco's late one afternoon when all the staff had dressed up for Halloween. Each time we turned a corner we were met with witches, skeletons, and a variety of different animals. They had made a huge effort to look scary and were jumping out at people in order to shock them. Obviously this was just harmless fun and all the other children loved it but to Connor they were very frightening. The staff thought he was screaming in delight but his fear was real. He raced up the aisles, hands clamped tightly over his ears in an attempt to block out the spooky noises being made. Being a really mean and nasty mummy, I just laughed, finding his reaction really amusing.

He still won't go anywhere near Santa at Christmas, preferring to wave from a safe distance instead, but at least he will look at him now without yelling, which is a big improvement on the past.

Inevitably, with all the comings and goings of family life, he did manage to escape one day. He can only have been about three, when to his delight, he found himself alone with an open front door. He couldn't open it at that age by himself, so this was an opportunity not to be missed. I had turned my back and someone had come in and forgotten to shut it. Within a split second I realised he had vanished and gave chase. I just managed to grab him as he reached the edge of the road when a huge lorry came hurtling past. Scooping him up in my arms I breathed a sigh of relief, convinced that he believed he was indestructible.

I still need to keep track of Connors' whereabouts at all times, even when we are in the house. Although he is a lot safer now than he used to be, and I can trust him in a room on his own for a short while without him wrecking something or putting himself in danger, he continues to require a very high degree of constant supervision. We can only ever truly relax when he is safely tucked up in bed and is fast asleep. After years of experience I have perfected the art of being able to tell exactly what he is doing even if he is out of my sight. Every noise, however small and inaudible, is an indication of where he is and what he is up to. I even recognise the different creaks of the door hinges to each room and can anticipate what his next move might be. Tom turned to me one day with a serious look on his face and said "Mum, you really do have eyes in the back of your head don't you?"

Connor has always loved going out and can get pretty angry and frustrated if kept in the house for long periods. He doesn't however realise that if he behaved better then we would be inclined to take him out more often. But having Tom to consider and with us all needing exercise, fresh air and contact with other human beings, we have had to take our chances over the years. We have braved dozens of trips with Connor to many different places. Some didn't go too badly, some were a total disaster; all were memorable for varying reasons.

When he was small, and the weather was reasonable, Tom and I would take him to outdoor play areas. I ensured we only visited those that were fenced in, and had to hover close to the gate to prevent an escape. If Tom needed me to push him on a swing or help him climb up something I would edge slowly over towards him, never daring to take my eyes off Connor for a second. He could move like lightning, and would be out and gone in the blink of an eye. He never, ever came back when you called him, so close monitoring was essential at all times. It was important never to lower your guard when out with Connor. He tended to play reasonably well at these places, but if it was busy he would push other children out of his way to get past. If a child was unfortunate enough to be sitting at the top of a slide when Connor reached the end of the ladder he would think nothing of shoving them down so he could take his turn. I stood at the bottom pleading with him to wait but he didn't understand what that meant. I knew he would completely ignore me, but had to look like I was trying. I soon got used to the other parents glares and cruel remarks. I don't think anyone believed me when I explained about his condition. He also used to commandeer any bikes or scooters that were left unsupervised. He assumed that they were there for anyone to play with, and had no clue that they belonged to other families. Even when we took our own with us, it wasn't the same as stealing someone else's. He was especially attracted to the pink sparkly bikes; it was a bonus if they had multicoloured streamers attached to the handlebars. He would pedal away furiously with a crying little girl chasing after him, desperate to retrieve her prized possession. Luckily most of the parents were reasonably understanding, and were happy to allow him to borrow the toys; the children were not so amused.

Again, as for every other aspect of our lives, Connor called the shots. When he had had enough he would leg back to the car, wanting to go home or on to somewhere else. Some days he would play for hours, other times he wouldn't last for more than ten minutes before screaming and throwing himself down on the ground. We could never tell why he did this, or what had triggered the reaction. All we knew was that the only solution was to give up and go home, which was tough on Tom when he had been looking forward to a good long play.

* * *

Indoor play places were a good option when the weather was bad, or it was too dark to stay outside. Although they are constructed to be ultra safe and child friendly, they presented a whole new range of problems for a child with Connors' excellent climbing abilities.

The main issues at first were his refusal to wear any form of identity bracelet or keep his socks on. Up to about the age of four I got round the sock issue by putting girls tights on under his trousers. Tom was horrified, but no one could see them, and it worked well for a while. He would become very annoyed at me, and pull hard at them in an attempt to get them off, but eventually gave up and played happily, until the day he decided enough was enough. Realising what I was doing, he kicked and screamed and flatly refused to let me put them on. I realised that I wasn't going to win this fight anymore and gave in graciously. The main reason he took his socks off was so that he could get a good grip on the slide. All the other children would be sliding down whilst Connor was attempting to climb up. He was knocked off his feet and sent flying to the bottom countless times, but this never deterred him from his goal. Maybe that was part of the fun, to see how far you could get before being crashed in to. This was a great game for Connor, but the staff were far from amused. Quite rightly, their role was to ensure the safety of all those who played there, and it was unacceptable to have a rogue child upsetting the balance of things. I lost count of the number of times I waded into ball ponds to hunt out lost socks and drag out a very angry little boy. There would follow a ten-minute wrestle on the floor to get them back on, and keep them on. I would attempt to remain calm, at least on the outside, while Connor screamed and yelled at me. People would turn to watch, never once offering the slightest ounce of assistance. I couldn't even use the threat of going home if he refused to comply, as he didn't understand what that meant. He would rush back in and seconds later the socks would be off again.

Most parents get to sit down and rest with a nice cup of tea at these places, as long as they glance up every now and then from their newspaper. I never even managed to sit, having to constantly be aware of Connors' every move. Each entry or exit point had to be monitored in case of an escape, and Tom was in charge of grabbing him before he got too far up the slide. I always explained his problems to the staff and they were sympathetic, but they couldn't allow him to compromise the safety of the other children there. He climbed up anything and everything, all the places that were staff only, Connor would venture into. He shinned up the poles that were holding up the structure, and his favourite was to clamber up the outside of the safety netting, right up to the top, and perch way above us peering down from near the ceiling. He used to rummage behind the counter, or wander into the kitchen to find something nice to eat. It was never relaxing going out to these kind of play areas, but the boys loved them and needed to get out for a while. It was always a relief to get home and close the door behind me; at last I could let my guard down just a little.

* * *

As we all love to go ten pin bowling, we decided to actually go as a whole family one day. I wasn't keen, envisaging a stressful afternoon out, but there would be enough of us to control him so how bad could it be? There was Frank, Jayne and Tom to help me, and we could take turns in chasing around after Connor. We had avoided trying this before, but he was around five now and was old enough to join in. I was surprised at how much interest he took, even allowing us to put on his bowling shoes without protest. I was amazed that he sat patiently waiting his turn; we had decided to put him last so that he could watch and learn what to do. When Connors' turn came I was actually starting to enjoy myself, he was behaving so well, and hadn't thrown a tantrum or run off for a change. He picked up a ball and walked over to the lane, as if he had played many times before. He made an attempt to throw it but the ball, being so heavy for him, just dropped like a stone, rolling along as if in slow motion. We were all willing it to keep going, but half way down it came to a grinding halt. Knowing that wasn't right, Connor decided the only option was to go and retrieve it himself. Before we could stop him he started to make his way carefully down the lane. Shouting him to come back was having no effect and he kept on edging further away. I panicked, and had visions of him not stopping and getting trapped in the heavy mechanism at the bottom of the alley. I saw no other choice but to follow him, in the hope that I could catch up before he made it to the end. Not realising how slippery it would be, I ran down the lane as fast as I could. Losing my footing I went flying right into him, knocking him over and pushing him even further away from me. Crawling on my hands and knees I eventually managed to reach him. After a few failed attempts at standing up again I crawled back up the lane, yanking Connor behind me by his clothes. Looking up I realised that the whole place had fallen silent; all eyes were on Connor and me. Nobody could quite believe what they were seeing. My face burning with embarrassment, I tried to ignore them and made it to the end. At last, being able to stand up, I realised that I had pulled a muscle in the top of my thigh.

Needless to say, I wasn't overly keen on a repeat performance, so we didn't go again for a while. On the next visit he wasn't at all interested in bowling, preferring to run around causing mayhem instead. Tom and I now go on our own, leaving Connor at home.

* * *

I have never felt so much shame as the day Connor broke into a strangers' house on the beach. I will remember the events of that day for as long as I live.

As I recall, it was a cold, dark, damp day; either autumn or early spring time. One of Toms' friends was going to the beach and had asked us to go along. I was wary, but this particular place, unlike others, had no high rocks for him to climb and nowhere for him to escape to. The only thing for miles was a single white house set on its own in the middle of a huge expanse of sand. We started off quite happily; Tom and his friend Alex were digging trenches and making sand castles. After joining them for about five minutes Connor decided it was time to run off and explore but as there was really nowhere for him to hide we let him go. We still had him in sight and the beach was deserted that day. Eventually as he got further and further away, I thought I'd better follow and persuade him to come back. Leaving Tom with Alex and his mum I set off after Connor, but when he saw me coming he changed direction and headed for the steep embankment at the back of the sand. When I finally found him he was already quite a way up, climbing through the dense mix of trees and prickly bushes, excited at the thought of being able to outrun me. The more I shouted the higher he went, thinking this was a great game. I struggled to push a path through the branches, slipping in my wet wellies. Eventually, within arm's reach, I lunged forward and grabbed his coat. He protested loudly at being caught, wriggling like a snake in an attempt to break free. Equally as determined, I held on tight and pulled him down and back to the beach. Once on solid ground I released my grip, figuring he wouldn't try to go up there again. He raced off angrily across the sand, roughly in the direction we had started from. Being quite exhausted by now I followed slowly behind. Seeing that Tom was heading our way I guessed he would intercept Connor before I caught them up. Moments later, I noticed Connor had turned and was now heading straight for the house. Starting to run I yelled to Tom to stop him if he could, but when I reached Tom Connor had completely disappeared. Keeping a short, but acceptable, distance from the property we hunted around in the trees and bushes but couldn't see him anywhere. We called his name but didn't want to shout too loudly for fear of disturbing anyone. Not wishing to trespass around the grounds of someone's home, I sent Tom to investigate, figuring it would look better if a child was nosing around rather than an adult. After two full circuits of the area, Tom came back alone. Whilst we were contemplating what to do next, a lady came out of the back door to inquire what we were doing; she had been startled by the sight of Tom rushing past the window. As I started to explain the situation she suddenly burst out crying and flung her arms around me. Rather shocked with this reaction, I instinctively hugged her back. We must have stayed there holding onto one another for a few minutes, with Tom staring at us with a look of utter confusion on his face. I didn't have a clue what to say, so just stood there in silence. Once the lady had calmed down enough to talk, she told us why she was so upset. Her husband had passed away the night before and she was, understandably, extremely distraught. I was absolutely mortified. I couldn't believe that we had rudely barged in on this family's life at a time of such immense grief. The last thing she needed was a strange child rampaging around her home. Just then her two grown up children came out to say that they had found a little boy running around upstairs. They asked if I wanted to go in and get him but I thought it better for them to do it instead, they had suffered quite enough intrusion for one day. When he finally appeared, oblivious to the distress he had caused, I grabbed him firmly by the hand. After a grovelling apology, not that it would ever be adequate enough for what he had done, we dragged Connor away.

Deciding it best to leave the beach, we headed for the café for a hot chocolate to warm us up. While waiting for the drinks Connor rushed off behind the counter to have a rummage through the ice cream cabinet. On his way back to the table he paused to study the sugar bowls that were laid out. We turned just in time to see him shovelling heaped spoonfuls of sugar into his mouth. As Tom darted off to stop him I just sat with my head in my hands, wondering how much more shame I could endure.

* * *

As we are lucky enough to have a large aquarium not far from our home we decided to take Connor there one day. He had been when he was younger and safely strapped in a buggy, but now he was around the age of five he would have to walk. I held tightly onto his hand determined to get our money's worth from the trip but he refused to cooperate. Breaking free he raced off, hurtling as fast as he could through each room, not even pausing to look at anything. This place is huge, with so many wonderful and interesting things to look at. There are open pools where you can see small rays and other types of fish, and loads of tanks containing many different variations of sea plants and animals. The main attraction is the enormous tank with a window the size of a whole wall, which is home to a whole array of creatures, including some very big scary looking sharks. You can also walk through a tunnel that is built into the tank and watch the fish swimming overhead. It is a great day out for both children and adults but Connor was interested in none of it. All he wanted to do was run, not taking a blind bit of notice of any of the animals, and I think completely unaware of why we were there. The only hint of interest he showed was in the shop at the end where he could choose a toy to take home. I had spent the whole afternoon chasing him around and had actually seen nothing.

\* \* \*

When he was around six, my parents suggested a visit to the safari park. We hadn't tried this with him before as we thought he might get too upset but as he would be locked in the car he would be easy to manage. As we drove through the large gates he started to get anxious, repeating to himself "I'm scared, I'm scared". We tried to reassure him but it didn't seem to work. Seeing an animal off in the distance he panicked. The seat belt was off in seconds and he was on the floor curled up in a ball with hands tightly gripping his ears. If he couldn't see them and, was able to block out any noise, then he figured he was safe. He was moaning and muttering to himself but he didn't seem too distressed so we decided to carry on. After about fifteen minutes on the floor I managed to coax him out with the promise of a drink. He calmed down and started looking out the window at the animals we were pointing to. He actually seemed to be enjoying it now, periodically having to check that the windows were still closed. He kept reaching up and feeling around the top of the glass for any gaps that might let in a creature or two. He appeared to realise that these animals could hurt him, but that he was safe inside the car.

* * *

Each year a local farm constructs a huge maze in their fields made from maize plants. The corn grows really high and even an adult struggles to see over the top. They open this up for families to go and try to navigate their way around the paths, and if you follow the instructions correctly, you should be able to make it all the way round and back to the beginning. Toms' friend Alex was going with his Mum and they called to see if we fancied joining them one morning. I was reluctant, wondering how Connor would react, but Janet promised to help out so we decided to go. It is great fun for the kids as there are clues to follow, carvings to rub, and puzzles to solve. Connor, of course, wasn't the least bit interested in any of that. All he wanted to do was run off in any direction. At first we managed to stop him just long enough to allow Tom and Alex time to find and resolve the clues. But every few minutes we managed to lose him again and would have to spend a while hunting him out. Eventually he legged off round another bend and we lost sight of him completely. He moved so fast that none of us could keep up and we decided to split up to widen the search. Not fancying getting lost in there myself I would periodically stretch my neck just high enough to shout to Janet over the top of the plants. After about ten minutes we caught up with Connor, who wasn't the least bit bothered about being out there on his own, he'd have run miles before wondering where the rest of us where. We had been going round in circles now for quite some time and were all getting a bit fed up by this point. Climbing on to a small wooden bridge we could see that we still had some way to go to get back to the farm if we followed the maze in the proper manner. Having done enough running for one day, and not relishing the thought of losing Connor again, we decided to abandon the paths and head in a straight line. As we pushed our way through the corn it was obvious others before us had done the same thing. There were gaps where there shouldn't be and some plants had been trampled down to the ground. It was a

162

relief to finally make it back, all of us being rather desperate for a trip to the bathroom by then.

* * *

Seven years ago Frank bought me a weekend at a health spa as a birthday gift. To get a night away from the boys was a rare treat for me, so my friend and I set off for the drive down south leaving Dad in charge. Frank phoned me on the Saturday morning to ask whether it was a good idea to take the boys on a ferry ride across the river. I cringed at the thought of what Connor could get up to but said I would leave the decision up to him. Frank decided to brave it and took them out for the afternoon; he called that night to let me know how it went. As I suspected it had been a rather disastrous day. Connor had, of course, wanted to do all the things he wasn't supposed to. He had spent the entire afternoon legging around the deck at full speed, attempted to enter areas roped off to the public and had even tried to climb over the side of the boat. As Frank recalled his stressful trip out I had to stifle a laugh. I wasn't the least bit surprised at his behaviour, that's what he was like every time I took him out. Frank, not having experienced this on his own before, was quite shocked. This was the first time he had taken the boys out alone.

* * *

Another favourite place to visit is the zoo. We have taken Connor there on a number of occasions over the years, hoping to get some kind of positive reaction from him. When he was very young, and still safely strapped in his buggy, things were relatively straightforward. I would wheel him around and position him so he had a good view of the exhibits but he never took the slightest bit of notice. Even from the ages of around three to five, when most children would be thrilled and excited at the sight of the animals, there was nothing. No interest in what type of animals they were, or what they were doing. I remember standing with Connor right next to the large glass window in the monkey house one day. There were dozens of them in there, all darting about excitedly at full speed. They were swinging from the trees on ropes, fighting each other, picking fleas out of each other's fur and eating them, and messing about with each other's bottoms. Connor just stood and stared straight ahead with a blank expression on his face. It was as if he couldn't even see them, like they didn't exist at all.

When he outgrew his pushchair, and was old enough to run free that's exactly what he did. We never got to actually stop for long enough to look at anything, and had to spend the whole time frantically chasing after him. With the zoo not being a cheap day out we really wanted to enjoy it at our leisure, but that was not allowed. On a busy day it was a nightmare as he was so fast and was easy to lose in the crowd. We decided that it wasn't worth taking him back there for a while, and didn't attempt it again until he had just turned six.

I gained permission from school to take him out for the day. As it was so full at the weekends and in school holidays, a quieter weekday was safer. We would stand a better chance of spotting him if he ran off. The teachers were very understanding, even putting the day down as an educational trip rather than just a holiday. My mum and I set off quite excited, with high hopes of this being a relatively stress free day. He tolerated waiting a few minutes in the queue, then headed straight for the shop located just inside the entrance. We reluctantly followed him in, normally preferring to leave this until the end of the day. Not wishing to instigate a tantrum this early on though, we decided to let him hunt around. I wasn't keen on lugging round some huge cuddly toy with me, but in the end he chose one thing only. It was a small rubber, very life like, replica of a flying eagle with floppy, outstretched wings and an elastic string to hold it with. He spent about ten minutes looking at all the toys in the store, and was clearly content with his final choice. He held on to it all that day and happily flew it around in the air, making some very realistic eagle sounds as he went.

We left the shop and decided to visit those animals that would be of most interest to Connor first. We had no idea how long his good mood would last, and wanted to try to see as much as we could before the novelty wore off. We also knew that once he spotted the outdoor play area we would be stuck there for quite some time, so this had to be avoided for as long as possible. The elephant enclosure was the closest to the entrance so we wandered over there first. Amazingly he actually showed some interest in these and studied them for a few minutes before legging off. We tried to steer him roughly in the directions we wanted to go, but realised in the end it was easier to let him go his own way and just follow. We weren't able to walk though, not even at a fast pace, it was running all the way. We raced at breakneck speed past the enclosures of those animals that were of little interest to Connor. We quickly realised that he only paused to look at the ones that he recognised from films or cartoons. Only able to catch a fleeting glance at most of the creatures, my Mum and I yelled to each other as we rushed by. "Did you see that?" was virtually all we could muster, as we struggled to catch our breath. You certainly got more than your fair share of exercise taking Connor out for the day. When we named the animals we noticed that he was more responsive, and would pause briefly to watch. The elephants were all called Dumbo, and there was the Lion King and Tigger. The penguins were from the film 'Happy Feet' and he tap danced happily while they swam around in the water.

The fish were all named Nemo, and we spent ages in the aquarium, going round in circles to revisit all the tanks over and over again. This became rather tedious after a while, but we were grateful for a chance to momentarily rest, and walk for a change. Connor was fascinated and seemed to be calmer and relaxed in here, watching them swimming around. Surprisingly, he was drawn to those fish that were dull and boring in colour, as opposed to the many brightly patterned ones. We spent a long time staring at a tank full of large black fish, slowly moving in unison back and forth in the same pattern. He repeatedly came back to these; not being able to see the attraction myself, I was obviously missing something.

When we came across a huge tiger, sat right up against the fence, Connor stopped to ask where his friend Winnie-The-Pooh was. After a few seconds to relax I stated that had he been in there at all, he had probably been eaten by now. Eventually we were all feeling rather tired and hungry so we made our way to the eating and play area. Connor had a wonderful time running and climbing around the large wooden ark. I had to climb in and locate him a few times when we had lost sight of him, but we knew he was quite safe as long as he didn't attempt any acrobatics. After an hour and a half we managed to persuade him to leave and carry on. We took a ride on the overhead railway, visited the panthers, and he even stayed still long enough to watch the sea lions being fed.

At various points throughout the day his enthusiasm waned, but we just promised to go home soon, and kept on going. This was the very first time he had lasted so long, and we were determined to make the most of it. After five exhausting, but happy, hours we gave in and made our way back to the car. He must have been so tired by then we even got past the shop without any fuss. My Mum and I were ecstatic. Apart from having to run so much and cope with a couple of short tantrums, we had, for once, had a brilliant day out.

# 11

## PATIENCE IS A VIRTUE

Many of us live our lives in the fast lane these days. Rushing around at a hundred miles an hour, trying to squeeze as much into each day as is humanly possible. We feel we need to be all things to all people, at all times. You strive to be a hard worker, a great parent, a loving partner and a loyal friend. You cook the meals, clean the house, walk the dog, rush to work, then feel you've let the world down if you're so much as one minute late to pick up your child at the school gate.

Have you ever felt frustrated when you take time out of your precious lunch break to visit the bank, only to find you're at the back of a very long queue? Have you lost your temper when you've dragged the whole family out of bed at 4am for an early morning flight, only to be told at the check in desk that there's a three-hour delay? Have you ever sworn out loud when you're stuck travelling at ten miles an hour behind a tractor on a narrow country road? I think most of us would agree that we've lost our rag at some point or another; we are only human after all. I get annoyed if I am late for anything, especially if someone else has caused it, but more often than not it is my own fault, so I only have myself to blame.

·   I think most parents of autistic children would agree that patience is one of the attributes you require truckloads of to cope with looking after them. I would challenge even the calmest of people not to have been frustrated with some of Connors' behaviour over the years. I think I'm a reasonably calm individual, often being described as extremely quiet, but even I have been pushed to the very limit by some of his antics in the past. He has driven me to the edge of despair, over and beyond the boundaries that I thought I could cope with.

There were a few occasions, years ago, when he wound me up so much I felt I needed to put some distance between us. I would put the boys out in the hallway and shut myself in the kitchen for a few minutes to calm down. They would be hammering on the door and crying. I was on the other side, crying too. They were upset because I had yelled, and wanted reassurance. I was upset because I was angry, not with them but with myself. I should be able to manage better, and not allow Connor to get to me so much, and I certainly shouldn't bring Tom into the equation. I felt like I was failing them as a mother, and neither of them deserved that. When a couple of minutes had elapsed, I would wipe away the tears and unlock the door. We would kiss and make up, and they would forget the episode in an instant, but I never forgave myself. I knew I needed to learn how to be calm and rational, but it was easier said than done in the circumstances.

I think I have improved a lot over time in the way I deal with Connor's behaviour. Either I am more used to it by now, and am less surprised or shocked by the things he does, or have built up resilience and become tougher in my approach. I know now that he is not really trying to be naughty; he just doesn't possess the intuition to understand the way things work. That is not to say though, that we have become in any way complacent, or let him get away with behaving badly, not for a second. We treat him the same as we treat Tom. Connor may still have very limited speech and understanding of our language, but he knows how to be polite, and can be taught right from wrong. He still makes mistakes on a daily basis and it is an ongoing battle, but we are confident that these lessons are gradually sinking in. He has to say please and thank you for everything he wants or receives. Being pleasant and courteous to our fellow human beings costs nothing, after all. Even Frank and I are always polite to each other whether the boys are there or not. It doesn't take much effort to offer someone a cup of tea, iron a much loved shirt, or buy his or her favourite treat once in a while.

Kids have to be allowed to grow up at their own pace and have room to breathe, but I can't abide cheeky or rude children, and that isn't accepted in our house. I am always pleased when other parents, or his teachers, comment on how well Tom behaves. They never have a bad word to say about him, and are often stating how polite and well mannered he is. I put this down to him being a nice, happy, contented young boy, and hope that we have taught him well. I also feel that he has been forced to learn to be a more caring and considerate individual because of Connor. Tom has struggled over the years to understand the problems Connor has, and has fought hard to come to terms with having a brother that is so different from his friends' siblings. He gets frustrated and angry like we all do, and needs his space to cool down. They will fight and argue and Connor calls Tom an 'EVIL CHILD', then ten minutes later I find them upstairs with Tom helping Connor to find a lost toy or reading him a favourite book. I think he has the patience of a saint, and copes tremendously well with Connor. He takes on the role of big brother very seriously, and doesn't realise how much he cares for him, and protects him from harm.

As much as we all need to be patient and considerate regarding Connors' differences, he himself must learn these lessons too. He has to learn that life is not all about him. That we are not all there just to cater to his demands and fulfil his desires. We are allowed to enjoy life too, and cannot run after him, or please him twenty-four hours a day. When he asks for a drink or a bite to eat he expects it to suddenly appear that very second, as if by magic. You are expected to drop everything and jump to his command every single time he wants something, and he gets angry when we don't immediately react. He doesn't understand that you might be busy and can't help him that very instant. He has absolutely no patience whatsoever, and will slam the cracker tin down right next to me at the dinner table while Frank and I are attempting to enjoy our evening meal in peace. Seconds later a knife will appear, then a plate, and then he goes back for the margarine tub. They will all be pushed virtually on top of my food, just to ram the point home, in case I still didn't get it. He will then trot off and make his own juice, at least he can do this by himself now, and expect to see a lovely plate of freshly coated crackers on his return. You will then be stared at, pestered and continually reminded until you give in and do what he wants.

He also can't comprehend why we won't take him shopping all the time. Given the opportunity he would happily visit his favourite toy stores every single day of his life, with no thought as to how expensive things are. He knows we need 'pennies' to spend in the shops, but has no clue what this actually means, and no idea how much hard work it takes to earn them. He asks to go all the time and when I say no to one he names another, then another, in the vain hope that this will gain a different response. If that fails he negotiates and says "tomorrow", assuming that if we can't afford to buy a toy today, then we will be able to by the morning.

Connor breaks his heart on Christmas Day when we refuse to visit McDonalds for his favourite chips. Even if we have been the day before he still can't understand that it is closed, and with all the will in the world there's nothing we can do to change that. One year we visited a friends' house for our dinner and had to endure an hour-long screaming fit with floods of tears pouring down his face. He refused to eat anything we offered him; he was so angry he couldn't get his own way. Maybe next Christmas we should buy some the night before, and then reheat them for his lunch the next day.

He has always struggled with waiting in queues. Regardless of where he is or how long the wait will be, it is just not acceptable in Connors' view. He doesn't see why you can't push your way to the front, trampling over anyone who gets in the way if necessary. After all life is meant to be lived at full speed, and there is no time to waste hanging around doing nothing.

Waiting in shops was dreadful, even if he was getting a new toy or DVD, he couldn't stand the thought of queuing to pay at the till. Reluctant to lose my place in the line I would attempt to hold on to him, but more often than not he would wriggle free and make a dash for the door, the unpaid item clutched tightly in his grasp. If Tom wasn't with me to grab him, I would have no choice other than to go and catch him before he set off the alarm at the front entrance. Dragging him back I would take my place at the back of the queue and start all over again. He would be screaming by now, terribly annoyed and furious with me. He often yelled at the top of his voice "HELP, I'M BEING KIDNAPPED!" and I would stand my ground and smile at the other shoppers as if nothing was amiss. We would slowly work our way up the queue with him squirming, shouting, and spluttering tears, while I held on for dear life. No one ever came to my rescue. No one thought to hold my place in the queue, or let me cut in front of them. No staff members ever offered to open up another till to serve us more quickly. People just glared or ignored us, and I would stand there mortified, my cheeks burning bright red, desperate not to catch anyone's eye. I always wish I'd had the strength and courage to shout out to these unhelpful souls, to let them know that he had a disability and wasn't the naughty little brat that he appeared to be, but I never once did. I didn't dare let down my guard for fear of what might happen if I allowed the floodgates to open.

If shopping wasn't bad enough, then airports were even worse, especially at particularly busy times when it could take hours to check in and get through security. Again he yelled the place down. Again, no one even attempted to try to help.

* * *

Have you even witnessed a child throwing a tantrum in a public place? Maybe in a shop or a park, at a zoo, or in an airport? What conclusions did you jump to about that child or the person with them? Did you immediately assume that the child was unruly, undisciplined, and out of control, or that

176

the carer was totally useless and incompetent? Did you tut loudly and walk off in disgust, positive for the fact that you would never allow your own children, or grandchildren to behave in this way? Did you ever pause to consider that there could be something wrong with that child and a good telling off and some harsh punishment would actually do more harm than good in those circumstances? Did you ever think that the person in charge of that child was unable to control its temper through no fault of their own? Did you walk away, or offer some help and support, and did you ever once wonder what it must feel like to have a child who kicks off like that?

Maybe next time you witness a scenario such as this, you could stop and think a while. Try to put yourself in their shoes and consider what that parent, carer, or whoever they are, has to cope with on a regular basis. Try to imagine how you would feel in a similar situation, and how you would want other people to react towards you. Even if you don't want to intervene or help in a practical way, you can be considerate, understanding, and compassionate. A small smile to show you care as you walk on by can go a really long way.

Remember that every stare, every negative comment, and every pointed finger is absolutely devastating, and is never forgotten.

# 12

## NAPPY WARS

It was a huge relief for everyone when we finally forced Connor out of his nappies in the summer he turned seven. I had heard stories of adults with autism who had never got the hang of using the toilet, and were destined to be in continence pads for the rest of their lives. I had horrendous visions of having to change Connor as an adult, and I admit I was more than a little worried. You don't expect a child to still be in a nappy after the age of around three, so imagine a seven year old. The bigger the child, the bigger the mess. It was also a massive step for him, an indication that he was slowly maturing, and another small, but very significant, battle won in the fight to give him some semblance of independence. If he was to grow up and lead any sort of normal life he had to get over this hurdle. I also saw this as a great achievement for us as his parents. Our whole life with Connor has been a constant and bloody battle of non-conformity, and despite our best efforts and tough approach we have rarely won. We were determined that this time he wasn't going to beat us.

Connor is the strongest willed person I have ever met. There is no room for negotiation, no blackmail tactics strong or clever enough to change his mind once it is firmly set on something. No particular toy or favourite food worthy enough of giving in for. Connor will only do what you want him to when he is good and ready, and not a moment before.

* * *

I had tried a few times to get him toilet trained in the past, with disastrous consequences. There were many attempts to put his underpants on without a nappy but each time he just screamed and ripped them off. He would get hysterical, as if they were actually burning his skin. Whether he hated the feel of the material or he just felt more secure in a nappy, I'll never know. But I do think that he was being lazy, why should he waste good playing time going to the bathroom when he could just fill his nappy wherever he was? I believe that given the choice, Connor would have quite happily stayed in them forever. He didn't see the need to be like everyone else, he doesn't bend to peer pressure like the rest of us. He had no idea that it was such an important stepping-stone in his development, or just how much it would significantly improve all our lives. Not to mention the fact that now even the largest size of nappy you could buy would barely fasten around him. He can't have been at all comfortable being squeezed tightly into them, but he appeared totally oblivious. It was a good job he was so skinny or the shop bought versions would never have fitted for so long.

The school nurse gave us some samples of larger varieties to try, pads meant for older children and adults, but they were either far too big and bulky, or just not good quality. They would blow up like a balloon with the slightest hint of liquid, and didn't seem to hold much in anyway; getting his clothes on over them was a work of art in itself. Connor may not eat much but he is a prolific drinker, chain drinking his juice throughout the day. It got to the stage where I had to change him at least once an hour, and it was getting ridiculous. Nearly all my time was taken up tending to his needs. It was a race to wrestle him to the floor, mop up the mess, then get a fresh pad on before he managed to escape. He thought it was a wonderful game to run off during this process, often before I had wiped him clean. I then had the job of trying to catch him before he sat down on anything and dirtied the furniture. It was great fun to be chased around the house with your mother in hot pursuit. I remember the sight of his little bare bottom darting from one room to the next in a bid to evade capture. Eventually I would corner him and frog march him back to the bathroom. It was an exhausting process that was to be repeated again within the hour, all day, every day, for years.

On average we were going through fifteen nappies a day, but as you can imagine the bladder of a seven year old has a much larger capacity than that of a two year old. We quickly learnt that if left any longer you were faced with some very soggy clothes, not to mention the beds, couches, and carpets as well.

Getting anyone to look after Connor was also a very big problem for us. Disregarding the fact that his behaviour was hard to cope with, having to face the prospect of changing the nappy of a large child did nothing to improve our prospects. It took a very brave babysitter to face this challenge, and there were few people either willing or able to help. It was essential that they were highly qualified, though not necessarily in the area of childcare. They had to be fully trained in the art of mortal combat, be an Olympic runner, and have a first class honours degree in patience and resilience. They had to be able to calmly coax him down from the tops of doors lampposts and trees, and not be fazed when he walked around the top of the banisters, climbed onto a roof, or tried to hang himself with a skipping rope.

For years the only person capable of managing him was his big sister, my stepdaughter, Jayne. My parents did their best to help too, but as he grew bigger, stronger, and faster, he was difficult for them to control. Jayne was brilliant. Her help proved invaluable to me, and without her support I think I would have gone completely mad. My stepson Guy was always enthusiastic to help out too but he drew the line at the nappy changing. He either had to wait until we came back, or in a dire emergency phone his girlfriend for assistance. It wasn't just the mess that put people off it was the fact that he was so strong it was impossible to get a tight grip on him to hold him still. If it hadn't been for Jayne and Guy we would have hardly ever got the chance to go out, and we'll forever be grateful for all they did.

Jayne has always been such a happy, bubbly, optimistic person and is to this day a terrific influence on the boys. There are not that many people who could have put up with the stress of caring for Connor and still come out laughing. She would constantly smile and make the best of things no matter what life threw at her. Even one particularly memorable night didn't put her off.

Frank and I were ready to go out, and our friends had just arrived for a pre-dinner drink. I was still attempting to catch the kids and get their pyjamas on, while the taxi driver was becoming increasingly impatient outside. The boys were chasing each other excitedly around the house with the dog in hot pursuit. As they all flew down the stairs and descended on the kitchen, we got a waft of something rather unpleasant that had obviously just been deposited into Connors' clean nappy. The dog, by now very hot and bothered with all the commotion, came panting over and promptly threw up her, thankfully still mainly undigested, evening meal right at Jayne's feet. With the taxi driver threatening to drive off, if we took any longer we just had to go and leave her to clean up the mess. Poor Jayne looked horrified. We thought it was hilarious; this kind of chaos was quite normal in our household.

* * *

I was actually pleasantly surprised at how easy it was to toilet train Connor that summer. We had decided to start the process the minute we got to our home in Spain. To start as we meant to go on. I was determined that when it was time to go home he would get back on that plane without wearing a nappy. Besides, if you've ever attempted a nappy

184

change in a plane toilet you will know what I mean. You can barely fit a tiny baby on the microscopic pull down shelf that masquerades as a changing table, let alone a large child, and are always guaranteed to hit turbulence at the most inconvenient of times. It requires a Masters degree in engineering to negotiate the removal of a full nappy off a moving target without spilling a drop.

At first he was reluctant to co-operate of course, this was no shock. He was more than happy to spend hours in his swimming trunks and go back and forth to the bathroom, but when the time came to get dressed all hell broke loose. If you dared to go anywhere near him with a pair of underpants he would just scream and rip them off. When I did manage to get them on he would rush to the cupboard, get a nappy out and shove it, still folded, down the front of his pants. Amazingly though, it only took a few days to break the cycle. He finally relented, and realising he wasn't going to win, gave in graciously. He was still wearing them for bed of course, but in the daytime, at the house, he was fine. Going out was our next target.

He was very nervous at first, I think he was scared that there wouldn't be a toilet to hand, or that he wouldn't make it there fast enough. I have to say that I was pretty worried about this too. But it wasn't as bad as we imagined. We tried at first to not go anywhere that wasn't familiar so we always knew where the restrooms were located. When we arrived at a restaurant I would take him to the bathroom straight away so he knew where to go. However, he still hasn't grasped the idea that you are supposed to actually enter the toilet and close the door before pulling down your pants and revealing all. We were in our favourite Chinese restaurant near our Spanish house one night when he suddenly jumped up and yelled "TOILET!" He ran off in the direction of the restroom, and things would have been fine if he hadn't pulled down his shorts first. The whole room got a great view of his little white bottom as it weaved its way through the tables before disappearing out of sight. Jayne, who happened to be with us that evening, was absolutely mortified and was ready to disown us. I just couldn't stop laughing.

He still had the odd accident, understandably so, but on the whole he was getting the hang of it. He did however take a liking to standing on the edge of the pool and weeing into the water. Maybe his logic was that you wee into water in the toilet so what's the difference? Besides, it was far too much effort to make the short journey to the bathroom that was

186

only a few yards away. As the rest of us didn't fancy swimming round in that he got a severe reprimand each time we caught him and has stopped doing it now. At first he also had problems knowing when to exit the pool when he needed a number two. Tom was given the unfortunate job of being 'poo' monitor, a role he actually took very seriously. Whenever he spotted something suspicious he would alert us and we would all peer down into the water hoping to find just a dead insect or a leaf, not the dreaded object. More often than not though Tom had been right, it was from Connor after all. As I hate to put my head under water Tom very kindly dived down with his mask on and took a net to retrieve the mess. I felt a bit guilty leaving such a horrible task up to him but he was a very willing participant. There were also instances when Connor had not made it out of the pool in time, but the contents were still contained in his swimming trunks. He would then scoop it up with his hands and run to throw it down the loo, dripping a trail of dirty water as he went. This was so disgusting. I then had to make sure that I mopped the floor before anyone trod in it and scrubbed his hands thoroughly. I am happy to report that he doesn't tend to do this now.

When summer was over and we flew home we were ecstatic. He had successfully managed to make a big step in his development, and I now didn't have to spend hours each day changing him. He arrived home in his underpants, the nappies being left behind.

\* \* \*

He still hasn't fully grasped the concept of privacy, but I am hopeful this will sink in eventually. All little boys get caught short when out sometimes and will nip discreetly behind a tree or bush for a quick pee. Connor though, hasn't learnt the art of hiding yet. He will just pull down his pants and go wherever he is, regardless of whether there is anyone watching. He would never do this inside, he knows not to do that, but out in the park, on the beach, or even in the garden he thinks nothing of baring his bits. His attitude seems to be "well the dog can do it so why can't I?"

He still has a bit of a way to go even now, but on the whole is getting the hang of things quite nicely. We have had some recent episodes that were rather unpleasant, but thankfully they are few and far between these days.

We happened to be in a large DIY store one afternoon when Connor suddenly decided he needed to wee. As it was attached to a supermarket, there were actually no facilities in the part of the building we were in. He yelled "TOILET!" and darted off in search of the bathroom before I could stop him. I turned the corner expecting to see him still standing there, but he was gone. He wasn't round the next corner either, or up the adjacent isle, I had lost him completely. After a frantic search of the surrounding area, I started to panic. A few minutes had passed by now, and I was no closer to finding him. Wondering if he had run outside I went over to the door but there was no sign of him in the car park. Ditching the trolley I rushed over to where the staff had congregated for a chat. It was early afternoon on a weekday, so the store was deserted, but not one of them offered to help me search for my missing son. Confirming they hadn't seen him they shrugged their shoulders and resumed their obviously very important conversation. Eventually I spotted him coming towards me from the area containing the showrooms. I was so relieved to find him, and then had the horrible thought of what he might have done if one of the rooms on display was a bathroom. He wouldn't know the difference between a toilet that was plumbed in and one that was just for show. Bearing in mind the unhelpful attitude of the staff, I didn't even bother to warn them of what might have just occurred. Grabbing Connors' hand we made a sharp exit, just in case.

* * *

If he messes up his pants he knows to put on a clean pair, although the lesson of putting the dirty ones in the wash basket hasn't sunk in yet. I often find soiled underpants strewn around the house, with varying amounts of mess inside them. Those that aren't too bad go straight in the washing machine; ones that are beyond saving end up in the bin.

We also went through the 'using too much tissue at one time' phase. There were quite a few occasions where I have had to get a stick out the garden and use it to retrieve half a ton of toilet paper blocking the pipe. I seem to get all the dirty jobs in our house! My sister drew the short straw one day when she visited with her two children. They were staying the night as they live a few hours' drive away, and I had just popped out to get a few things for our dinner. Of course, the second I left the house Connor decided he needed the loo. Going in a few minutes later to check up on him, she made a shocking discovery. He had rammed in a whole roll of toilet paper and had tried to flush it down. With the water having nowhere else to go, it was rapidly rising to the top. Facing the prospect of a flooded bathroom she made the ultimate sacrifice, she pulled up her sleeves and waded in. On hearing the story when I returned from the shops, we decided that I should be the one to cook the tea that night.

If that sounds gross though, it's nothing to what we faced when he was much younger. Between the ages of around two to five he often seemed to poo in the middle of the night. This would have been fine if he had stayed asleep or come to wake me up, but he did neither of these things. Instead, he decided to get up, scoop the contents out of his nappy and smear it anywhere he could find. Nowhere was immune from this vile attempt to get the mess off his hands. The bed covers, furniture, carpet, walls, radiator, and the mirror on the wall by his bed, all succumbed to this nightly ritual. Even more disgustingly, he would then climb back into bed and go to sleep. I would then be woken in the early hours of the morning by a vile odour emanating from his room. As you can imagine, the scene I was confronted with was horribly unpleasant, and it took a good hour or more to clean up both him and the mess. The whole house reeked, and I was forced to fling open all the windows in an attempt to clear the stench. I lost count of the number of baths I ran, and bed covers I washed in the middle of the night. I feel physically sick now even just thinking about it!

I can't imagine, with his heightened senses, just how on earth he could stand the smell, but we are immensely relieved that this is something he eventually stopped doing.

# 13

## AUTISM, THE FACTS OR THE FICTION?

It took a very long time, but eventually I had to stop fretting over the possible reasons why Connor had his autism. That's not to say those reasons aren't important, of course they are, but mulling them over in my head, time and time again, was doing more harm than good. I think in the early days, Frank and I both blamed ourselves, but never each other, thank goodness. We didn't know what to think, who to turn to, or where we went from there. It was a complete roller coaster of mixed emotions, feeling reasonably positive one day, to sick to the pit of your stomach the next. I spent years in a state of high emotion, bursting out into floods of tears at the slightest of things. Anything relating to Connor was enough to set me off.

We felt very let down by the system as a whole. Many people were assigned to his care, all with different skills, areas of expertise, and ways of working. They came round regularly to assess him and get updates on his progress, if any. All were extremely diligent and caring, and it helped me to be able to rant and rave for an hour at a time about his terrible behaviour to someone who supposedly understood. But we never really got very far, a lot of what was discussed seemed to be based on individuals' own opinions, rather than any scientifically based formulas. In fact, at times these visits made things even worse as some gave us conflicting information and you were left unsure as to who to believe. Sadly though, that's what this disability is all about - uncertainty, confusion, and massive changes in behaviour patterns. We have learnt most of what we know through our own research, as have many of the other parents I have spoken to. The census of opinion is that if you want something done, then you have to do it for yourself. If you need to learn something, you find it out yourself. There is no one there to guide you through the mess and mayhem this condition can bring to your life.

It was a very scary time for us when we received Connors' diagnosis. We were bombarded from all directions with statistics, facts, probabilities, and possibilities. There were the general list of signs and signals to look out for when determining whether a person has this disability. I had to look up what the 'triad of impairments' actually meant, as I hadn't heard of it before. Basically, it is a term to explain the three areas where the person has the most difficulties:

Social interaction
Social communication
Imagination

There are also certain characteristics and behaviour patterns that are associated with autism. Although it varies widely, as to how many or how few of these traits a person might have:

Repetitive Behaviour
This could be repeated flapping of the hands, or a certain object. Rituals are common, such as having to do things the same way each time, or having to use the same route to get somewhere. Arranging objects in lines or particular patterns, for example toy cars. Having the need to collect odd things. Developing an obsessive interest in one favourite topic and talking about it constantly.
Challenging Behaviour
Running away, biting, screaming, kicking, or other socially unacceptable habits. They may say the

wrong things, not realising they can hurt other people's feelings. Some find it very hard to cope with changes in their routine, and need familiarity to remain calm.

Interacting With Others

Poor eye contact is often associated with autism, as is limited or no speech. They may find it difficult to read other people's faces, not understanding the meaning of facial expressions, i.e. if someone is happy, sad, angry or frightened. Some children prefer adult company as opposed to other children, and might be happier playing alone rather than with someone else. Some will indicate their needs by taking the hand of an adult to a desired place or object, rather than use speech to relay the message.

It was easy to see which of the characteristics Connor was displaying, but the outlook for the future remained very uncertain. No one could guess how he might develop, or what he would be like as he grew up. The possibilities were endless, and no one could wave a magic wand to make it all better.

Not only did we have to come to terms with being told our three year old had a lifelong disability, we were bombarded with negativity from all directions. Nobody was prepared to say anything positive, or give us any indication that we may see some improvements over time. Coping with him on a daily basis was hard enough; digesting all the information was an absolute nightmare.

We were told that he might decide to talk, but might not. He may learn to read and write, but possibly not. He might never know who his family members are, or even comprehend that we are related to him at all. He would probably be unable to show emotion, express his desires, or understand the needs of those around him. He may never have the ability to learn social skills or show any form of imagination; will never live independently and will require round the clock care for the rest of his life. If we get really desperate, there may possibly be some respite care available when he is older to give the rest of us a break.

All these statements came as a shocking blow. I knew he was very difficult, but I was still clinging to the vague hope that things would slowly improve to some degree, as he grew bigger. Each time he said a new word, showed that he understood a human emotion, or made the slightest of improvements, I would jump up and down excitedly. On their next visit I would gloat to the health care workers about his small, but very significant, achievement, expecting just a little show of support or enthusiasm. A tiny indication that we were finally heading in the right direction was all I was searching for. Instead I got nothing. On each occasion I was met with a wall of silence. The best I could hope for was a sympathetic smile and a slow, knowing nod of the head; they had seen it all before, was their reaction. They would gently point out that these small steps were actually no indication that things were improving at all; he may never repeat the word or the gesture ever again. He could even regress backwards at any time and lose the few skills he had gained up to now. Every time I saw a glimmer of hope I was shot back down. Every time I dared to believe that there was light at the end of the tunnel, I was deflated. Every time I had faith, my dreams were shattered. There were never any signs of optimism, or words of comfort, only quiet sympathy and sorrow. None of this helped me bond with Connor, and threatened to make an already fragile relationship even more unstable. It was impossible for me to enjoy my child when the days were filled with conflict, and he rarely slept at night. I seriously questioned my abilities as a parent, and my self-esteem and confidence plummeted. I felt there was no one willing to help me, or even just guide me in the right direction. I appreciate they can't give false hopes, that would be very unprofessional and downright wrong, but surely the odd word of encouragement could do no harm?

* * *

During one of his early annual reviews with the community paediatrician we enquired about our chances of having another child with the same condition. Not that we were planning on having any more, we felt we had quite enough on our plate as it was, but needed to know regardless. If, in the future, we decided to consider the possibility of extending our family, we wanted to be able to make an informed decision, to take a calculated risk rather than a stab in the dark. Obviously as there are no tests for autism, this would only be a percentage risk factor; there was still no way of knowing for sure. Even if you get a one in a million chance, you could still be that one out of a million. The doctor informed us that as things were now, we stood a ten percent chance of having another autistic child, but if Connor was found to have Fragile X Syndrome, then any future child of ours would have it too. The only good thing was that a simple blood test would either confirm this or rule it out. We decided to go ahead, not really wanting to put Connor through any unnecessary discomfort, but figuring that a quick needle in the arm wouldn't be so bad.

Unfortunately, it didn't go quite as smoothly as planned.

We were assured that the nurse who would carry out the procedure was experienced in dealing with special needs children and it would be fast and relatively painless for Connor, causing him the least amount of distress possible. Not wanting to face this alone, Frank and I went along together and arrived at the school for a short briefing before Connor was brought from the classroom. The school nurse was there as well, and we all knew who was going to do what in advance. When he came into the room he knew something was amiss, he seemed comforted by the fact that mum and dad were there, but confused with all the fuss. His little hands had been taped up earlier to allow the anaesthetic cream to work, and I felt so sorry for him. The plan was that I held him still on my knee while the blood was extracted. Yeh, right. This is a child who won't sit still to eat, let alone allow some strange woman to stick scary needles into him. He freaked out big time, even before they had begun. I held on for dear life, there was no way on earth I could hold his body still, let alone his hand. The wonderful, specialist nurse who was supposed to be an expert in these situations just stood there looking shocked. She couldn't even manage to get a vein up, and

Connor was getting more and more agitated by the second. Frank, having done this hundreds of times in his career, suggested he could try, so he held Connors hand in a tight grip so the needle could be inserted. As he held on, the nurse made her first attempt to retrieve the blood. I couldn't see what was going on as my face was pushed hard against Connors' back in my effort to keep him on my lap. All I could hear was him screaming wildly in my ears, and I prayed for it to be over quickly. After what seemed like an eternity, everyone else let go. I sat up relieved, it had been a traumatic experience for poor Connor but at least it was over. Sadly though, it wasn't. The 'expert' nurse had managed to get not one drop out of his left hand, so now they needed to try with the right. I was mortified. It took all my efforts to stop the tears from pouring down my face. I felt like grabbing him up and running away; why were we putting him through this hell? Eventually they got what they needed out of his other hand. Even the school nurse appeared shocked and upset after all the trauma. Connor was hysterical and we took him back to class to calm down. I was desperate to take him home as I thought he'd been through enough, but the teachers didn't want his day interrupted any further and wouldn't let us. When it was time to leave I got a big hug and a kiss on the cheek. He had apparently forgiven me for what we had done, but Frank wasn't so lucky. When he went over to say goodbye he was greeted with a rather different reaction. Connor pulled away from him with a look of hatred I'd never seen before, he obviously blamed his dad for what had happened, and wasn't ready to forgive just yet. We went on our way, Frank looking visibly distraught and unable to speak with the lump in his throat.

* * *

As autism seems to be getting more and more common, it is imperative that we discover the cause or causes. The current level of children being diagnosed in the UK is around one in every hundred, and we need to protect our future generations if at all possible. Frank, always being more pro-active than reactive, decided to look further afield. Working all over the world in the medical business, he was more familiar with the terms used and tests available than I was. He studied institutions in America that claim to have substantially altered some children's' behaviours and increased their abilities. It so happened that he was on a flight to the US one day, and found himself sat next to someone connected with one of these places. They directed him to a laboratory run by highly respected and reputable doctors, who could run a whole host of tests if we collected the necessary samples from Connor. It was going to cost a lot of money, around a thousand UK pounds, but desperate for some answers, we agreed to go ahead. The first hurdle was obtaining the various bodily secretions needed, namely blood, urine, stools and hair. Sounds relatively easy I know, but for a child whose bowel movements swung from severe diarrhoea to complete constipation from one day to the next, it was not so straightforward. It was imperative that these samples were collected within a two to three day window, be maintained at certain temperatures, and shipped to the lab surrounded by ice packs to keep them fresh. If any of them degenerated they would be deemed useless and have to be destroyed. We received a box housing all the materials and containers we would need. I put the ice packs in the freezer, and studied the instruction leaflets carefully. We only had one shot at this, and had to get it right first time. We started the process at the weekend so that the content of his nappies could be closely monitored. The plan was to get all the samples we needed by Sunday night, with the exception of the blood. We had pre warned our GP who was more than willing to help us, and had made an appointment for the Monday morning.

Having a child with aspergers' syndrome meant he was very sympathetic to our cause. Connors' hair had been left to grow longer than usual, as they required at least an inch long chunk from the back of his neck. This was obtained fairly easily and was inserted into a bag, sealed, and his details written on the outside. The urine was caught with the use of a potty and could be stored in the fridge in a sealed bottle; kept cold this was fine for a few days. The next hurdle was the stool sample. It needed to be solid, but of course as sods law prevails, he was loose all weekend and we had nothing we could use. Monday morning came along with its own challenges. To make it less painful for Connor to have his blood taken we needed to put analgesic cream on the back of both his hands and a dressing over it to prevent him from wiping it off. Sounds straightforward I know, but not for a child who hates with a passion anything foreign being put on his skin, and detests even the smallest of plasters. After our disastrous encounter at school, I was dreading this day. I couldn't face a repeat performance, and didn't want to put him through any more pain. As it happened though, Connor was, amazingly, extremely cooperative, and the doctor did an excellent job at extracting the blood quickly and painlessly. It then had to be spun in a centrifuge to separate out the cells, and was taken home to be stored in the fridge. By Wednesday morning we had all the samples required for the tests. They were all packed carefully in their respective packages and sent on their journey to the states.

When we received the results we set up a telephone conference call with the laboratory so they could interpret these for us. It was found he had high levels of certain elements such as aluminium and lead, and lower than usual levels of sodium, potassium, manganese, molybdenum, selenium and cobalt. It was also noted that Connor had a moderate intolerance to casein, milk, oat, tomato and whey. The organic acid profile showed high levels of 3-oxoglutaric, oxalic and the neurotransmitter VMA. I was still quite confused as to what these results actually indicated and what, if anything, needed to be done about them. It was suggested that we try and modify his diet and give certain supplements and vitamins, but for a child whose food intake was already virtually non-existent, and who wouldn't even contemplate taking a tiny sip of Calpol, this was not going to be easy. I really felt none the wiser after spending a lot of money, and we took these results to our own doctors but they didn't know what to make of them either. We even had the water supplier out to test the levels of lead in our pipes, but this came back as negligible. In America they deliver a therapy called Chelation, which removes the heavy metals from the body and is reported to help the concentration in people like Connor, but this does not seem to be done in the UK. Apparently our doctors do not deem it to be a safe procedure.

We are still to this day, trying to find someone in this country that can both interpret these results for us, and suggest any necessary treatments. We don't know if having these various amounts of metals and other substances in his body is doing any harm, and whether there would be any benefit in taking this further. We need someone to advise us and point us in the right direction.

* * *

Over the years I have read so many stories about peoples beliefs as to why their child has autism and what can be done to reduce the symptoms. Some believe that there were no signs until the MMR vaccination was given, and are utterly convinced that this was the cause. I have no idea if this is true or not, and cannot blame that for Connor as we chose not to give him that particular jab, but I think parents who do believe this should have their cases taken seriously. There have been reports of autism being partly hereditary and partly environmental, but what exactly that is supposed to mean is anyone's guess. Could it be that there are a number of factors to consider that if a child has a predisposition to the condition then coming into contact with something could either trigger or exacerbate the symptoms? One thing we would like to know is how Connor came to have these high levels of metals in his system, and what they are doing to his body. We have asked whether these have come from the vaccines he had as a baby, at two, three and four months old, but no one seems willing or able to answer us. Was he born with them or have they been ingested somehow? Why is it that so many autistic people have problems with their gut, and what is the relationship between a learning disorder and intestinal issues? I believe that until we have discovered the definitive cause or causes, then nothing should be discounted or dismissed. That every angle should be considered, every avenue explored, every parent be given the chance to be heard. Dr Andrew Wakefield was brave enough to stand up and voice his concerns, for his efforts he was struck off and is now unable to practise medicine in the UK. From what I have read he was only trying to open up a debate on the possibility of a link between the MMR vaccine and autism, he was not actually saying that a link had been found, and did not intend to cause panic. But that was enough; the damage was done and the government closed ranks.

As a parent I would like to know what has caused Connors' autism for the sake of our future generations, and for my own peace of mind. It is too late now to reverse what has happened to us, but I would like to think that Jayne, Guy and Tom could possibly be spared the heartache Frank and I have gone through.

\* \* \*

Connor still struggles on a daily basis with his social interaction and communication skills and with his behaviour, but he shows great strength in other areas. His imagination and sense of humour are amazing, and he understands human emotions just as well as we do.

Years ago, before he spoke at all, I was crying in the kitchen, frustrated and exhausted as usual, and struggling to cope with him. Connor walked into the room and just stood there in silence, gazing at my face. He slowly walked over, and without uttering a word he gently wiped away a tear that was falling down my cheek. Taking one last look he turned and left as quietly as he had entered. I stared after him in shock. I couldn't believe that this child, who was not supposed to understand about feelings, had shown such compassion. He could of course just not have liked my wet face and been attempting to dry it, but I prefer to go with the previous version. It was the first time he had displayed a caring side and I was blown away.

# 14

## THE GHOST OF HOLIDAYS PAST

I am extremely lucky to have such wonderful, understanding parents. They have always gone out of their way to help me with Connor and for that alone I will forever be immensely grateful. When the boys were little and Frank was travelling, we spent many happy weekends at their house. They have a very long garden with trees; bushes and the garden shed blocking the view from the house. Connor liked nothing better than spending hours running up and down the full length of it, disappearing off into the distance and out of sight. He never seemed to tire or get fed up of this game. Not being able to trust him being alone for more than a few seconds, we had to take it in turns to chase after him. You couldn't dare give him the opportunity to climb up a tree, eat something vile, or clamber over the fence into next door. At this age he never came back when you called him, never even paused to get his breath back, he would just keep on going wherever he was, and you had no choice but to follow.

When we braved a trip to the park we all had to be ready. Before the front door was opened we had to ensure that our footwear was suitable for an Olympic sprint. The second he got outside he would run. I would attempt to keep up with him, with my Mum, Dad and Tom legging a few yards behind. We would run all the way there, all round the park, then all the way back. There was never any question of Connor walking nicely at your side in those days. He never walked anywhere, not even round the house. It was either running at full speed or standing still, nothing in between, and he was fast. Very, very fast. Even in the evenings he didn't sit down. He loved to stand on the back of their armchair and fling himself wildly off across the living room. My poor Dad was demented, panicking in case Connor hurt himself. He also liked nothing better than sliding down their glass banister, and nearly crashing through the glass front door. By the time we went home on Sunday night we were all exhausted. My parents waved us goodbye, then spent the next few days recovering from all the trauma.

* * *

Surprisingly though, they were still up for spending a week or two with us each summer at a caravan park in North Wales. As they had to virtually pass my house to get there, it was only sensible for them to call for us on the way. Of course, we were never ready; I would still be forcing yet more luggage into an already overcrowded car. I have never been very good at travelling light. Everything had to go, books, toys, footballs, board games, tennis racquets, buckets and spades, puzzles, pens and paper, videos, in fact anything I could think of to keep the boys amused. This must be one of the few countries in the world where you need to take Wellington boots and flip-flops, together with thick woolly jumpers and flimsy bikinis on the same holiday. Eventually, when there was not a speck of room left, we went on our way. I chose to follow my Dad, as with me driving in front we'd have been lost within a mile. We would attempt to make it all the way without stopping as Connor was very unpredictable in strange places, but inevitably there were occasions when a quick toilet break became a necessity.

We first started visiting caravan parks when Connor was very young. Obviously before he could walk he was easier to control. As he didn't sleep much we had some extremely long days, but we still managed to enjoy the break. He took his very first steps on the grass in front of the caravan just weeks before he turned one. We were all pleased that we had witnessed this great moment in history, but knew now that there was trouble ahead.

Connors' mission in life has always been to escape, from wherever he was, or whomever he was with. He did this at home, and being away in a strange, unfamiliar environment didn't deter him either. The fact that there are dangers around every corner never entered Connors' head at all. If he fancied a wander, or was angry about something, this made him more determined than ever to teach us a lesson. We were always careful, making sure that at least one of us had our eye on him, but inevitably there were times when he succeeded to evade us. Once he was a competent walker, he quickly learned how to open doors. Unfortunately, caravans can't be locked with a key from the inside; there is just a small catch to secure the door. Seizing his opportunity one day when our backs were turned, he undid the catch and ran. We were busy making dinner, and didn't realise what had happened until we heard the screech of brakes just outside. I turned to where Connor had been standing just seconds earlier, and realised with horror that he'd gone. With fear washing over me I flew down the steps and ran into the road. We were right on a bend at the end of a row, not the best location to be in at all. I was greeted with the sight of Connor calmly standing in front of a car, his hands stroking the bonnet. He wasn't in the least bit phased, having no clue whatsoever that had the driver not seen him, or had been going any faster, he probably would have been killed outright. Picking him up, I walked back inside, my heart thumping hard in my chest.

Each year we persevered, hoping that as he grew older he would become more cooperative and easier to cope with. Sadly, this wasn't the case, in fact the bigger he got, the harder he was to manage. We spent many long days chasing after him up and down beaches; he was never content to just sit and play in the sand, preferring to run for miles instead. Of course, it wasn't safe to let him go off alone, so we had to take it in turns to leg after him. He would run into the sea whatever the temperature of the water; it could be freezing cold but it didn't deter him one bit. On one particularly chilly day he went in fully clothed and ended up sopping wet from the waist down. As he was still in nappies then, this filled up and expanded to many times its normal size. On the walk back to the site, it slowly slid down his legs, swaying from side to side, and ended up hanging down by his ankles by the time we reached the caravan. He stopped outside the door, looked down, and without a word just stepped out of the nappy and carried on as if it was quite normal.

On one occasion we were on a long beach with high sand dunes running the length of it. Our attempts to keep Connor away were futile, and he thought it was wonderful fun to chase up and down them at full speed. Being small, light and agile, he was able to easily skim across the sand with ease, my Mum and I were not so agile and were decidedly heavier. As the hills were pretty steep, we couldn't see Connor from the beach, so decided we had to follow and keep track of him. We couldn't trust him not to run away, and didn't know if there were any strangers lurking around. After a good thirty to forty minutes chasing up and down my Mum and I were exhausted, it was hard work when your feet constantly sank in the soft sand. In the end Tom stepped in and managed to catch hold of Connor, we left soon after, not an ounce of energy remaining to run any further.

The holiday parks we visited were large, housing hundreds of mobile homes and purpose built cabins. There were plenty of facilities on site too, with indoor pools, play areas and huge rooms full of games machines. During the school holidays though, the places were packed to the brim with tons of people, making it much harder to keep your eye on a child intent on escape. Wherever we went it was crowded, and it was very easy for Connor to slip out of sight. My Mum, Dad and I would have to spend hours split up, one of us attempting to keep up with him, the others guarding the entry and exit doors to prevent a breakout. Using the swimming pools proved a nightmare too, as he insisted on running on the wet, slippery tiles. We had no way of stopping him; he never took a blind bit of notice when being told off, but the lifeguards went berserk, so we had to keep the number of visits to the bare minimum.

One summer we decided to rent a cottage on the Welsh island of Anglesey, just for a change. We figured it might be a little easier than having to control Connor in a big holiday park full of people. The house had a narrow, long, steep drive with high brick walls on either side. We had been assured that there was plenty of room at the top to turn a car around; it was impossible to reverse out backwards. It took us a while to even find the place, as the entrance resembled nothing more than a muddy dirt track, and we were convinced that it couldn't possibly be the way to the cottage. Eventually we realised we were in the right place and made our way slowly up the path. Being in reasonably large cars, my Dad and I edged our way up, with only inches to spare between us, and the solid walls. On reaching the top my heart sank; the 'large parking area' turned out to be tiny, barely big enough to park two cars, let alone turn them around. Not being a confident driver at the best of times, I was not impressed. The cottage itself was pretty old, full of ancient furniture, and really in need of a fresh coat of paint, but we decided to make the most of things and settled in as best we could. We spent the week visiting various beaches, farms etc, with Connor being his usual challenging self. The weather wasn't great though, and when it rained the front path turned into a mud bath, making getting in and out that much harder. You awoke in the morning to the cows staring through the bedroom window, and we were plagued by a three-legged dog that insisted on hanging out by the front door, and pooing all over the grass outside. This wasn't terribly hygienic, especially as the boys wanted to play out on the lawn. My niece Melissa had come with us too, and she and Tom spent most nights hiding under the covers, convinced the place was haunted due to all the creaks and rattles that come with sleeping in an old property. They all ended up in one bedroom, no one being brave enough to stay in a room on their own. In one bedroom there was a rickety old wooden wardrobe, rather similar to the one in the Wallace and Gromit animation film 'The Wrong Trousers'. Recognising this, Connor spent many happy hours imitating the scene where Wallace gets locked inside and stamps loudly up and down in an attempt to escape. We were a little worried he might break through the bottom of the floor, but luckily it was tougher than it looked.

These weeks away with Connor were quite stressful, but we always managed to maintain our sense of humour and laugh about it all, although I think my parents breathed a sigh of relief when it was finally time to go home.

# 15

## THE TOLL IT TAKES

Inevitably in our lives we have to face up to certain events or situations that we find distressing. Many things can cause us to feel sad, such as a relationship breakdown, losing a job, or the passing of a loved one. We all have our own ways of dealing with things, and our own defence mechanisms to help us to cope. Never assume that you know how someone else feels in a similar situation. You may know how you'd feel, but you don't live in the mind of that other person. Eventually we pick ourselves up and move on with our lives, but a particularly upsetting episode can take its toll in some way or another.

Living with autism can put a tremendous strain on the whole family. Everyone is affected to some degree; no one is immune to the pressures this condition brings. On a day-to-day basis, it has been Tom and I that have suffered the most in the past. As Frank has worked away so much he was partly removed from the constant battles and temper tantrums we constantly endured. He did however, get a condensed down version of events over the phone each night, with me ranting on about how badly behaved Connor had been that day. I'm sure this was the last thing he needed after a long day working, having to come back to a lonely hotel room with only one English Channel on the TV, and me yelling down the phone. I think we both suffer an equal amount of mental stress over Connor, but that we deal with it in different ways. I am more open and can show my feelings easily, Frank is more reserved, but that doesn't mean that the emotions aren't there.

\* \* \*

I am saddened, but not at all shocked, by the statistics of family breakdowns as a result of having an autistic child. It is reported that a massive eighty five per cent of couples end up having to part, unable to cope with the immense pressure heaped upon their relationship with one another. It is very understandable in the circumstances, but equally so terribly tragic. Inevitably, this means that one or both of those parents will have to learn to cope with their child alone, causing the stress levels to rise even further. It is a sad end to what might have once been a close and loving partnership, and even worse if there are other children involved too. Everyone loses out; there are no winners in this situation.

* * *

Having children is a huge, but natural, step in many peoples' lives. All young children can, at times, be demanding, exhausting and a drain on your energy. I am sure that children are the cause of many a spat between partners and can cause tension within a relationship, but you can put them to bed, relax, open a bottle of wine and enjoy an evening together, alone. This is unheard of in our house. It is only within the last year that we have been able to get Connor into bed at a reasonable hour. I will read him a story or two and then we have a cuddle, and if we are lucky he might drop off to sleep. By now though it can be ten o'clock, and the evening has already gone. There was never any question of bath and bed by seven thirty as most young children do. Connor slept very little when he was younger, often only needing a few hours a night. When he reached six he was sleeping for around seven hours, but even that isn't very much. You had to choose between putting him to bed early and waking up in the early hours, or going to bed late and lasting until six in the morning. Neither option was very attractive, an evening with little sleep, or no evening, but enough sleep to be able to function the next day. We felt we had to opt for the second choice, but it meant that Connor stayed up until eleven or twelve at night, every night. We weren't forcing him to stay awake, he had plenty of energy and kept on going until we finally forced him to lie in bed and put out the light. He would get back up and put the light back on numerous times in the night and we'd have to go in and put him back to bed. Of course, these late nights affected Tom's sleep patterns too, and he often ended up in bed far later than he really should have been. I even told his teachers what home life was like, so that they knew the reasons why he was so tired in the daytime.

Frank and I rarely argue about anything, but we have had the odd heated row over Connor in the past. Not that we have disagreed over many things, we are usually open to listen to each other's point of view, but sheer exhaustion and frustration can turn something small into something explosive.

* * *

It is so easy to take things for granted in this life. Like the ability to be able to do whatever you want whenever you want to do it, within reason of course. Having a 'quality family life' isn't something we can take for granted. In fact, for the most part, we have no family life together at all. Even a dinner out is usually a nightmare as he refuses to stay at the table and won't eat anything on offer. If we take his portable DVD player you have a chance of him sitting for a limited time period, but I use the word 'sitting' rather loosely. It is more like bouncing, jumping and periodically crawling under the table. He will sing along loudly to a song on his player, not caring that the whole restaurant can hear him too. Shushing him never works; he finds it physically impossible to be calm or quiet. If we visit somewhere there is an outdoor play area then he is happy, but he refuses to come inside to eat and we can't leave him unattended outside. We have to take turns in staying with him, or drag him in kicking and screaming. More often than not I just refuse to go anywhere in the first place, not being prepared to face the stress it causes.

We can go to watch a movie now, but only the ones Connor chooses. Inevitably, he prefers those which neither Frank nor Tom are interested in, so most of the time we go alone.

We can't go to our local bowling alley either as there is a large indoor play area nearby which he adores. Tom has decided that he is getting a little too old to play there now and gets bored quickly, but once Connor has seen the sign there is no persuading him to go anywhere else. If we attempted to go bowling but not enter the play place all hell would break loose. There would be a very loud lie down protest in the car park and the outing would have to be abandoned completely. Having learnt the hard way that Connors mind cannot be changed, Tom and I again go alone. Sometimes we ring up one of his friends to come along too, but it is frustrating that we can't just go out as a whole family and have fun together.

Many of Toms' classmates go on holidays to 'Disneyland' or 'Center Parcs', built specifically for the whole family to enjoy. We have successfully avoided these types of places, as they are very busy, noisy and crowded. Not the kind of atmosphere that Connor would be easy to control in, but it doesn't seem fair on Tom that he has to miss out on this kind of vacation.

* * *

As much as my life is affected by Connors' autism, it is Tom that concerns me the most. True, there are some things that they can do together, and I think that despite everything he does love him, but it is very hard for him to cope at times. He gets frustrated and angry, and says he can't wait to grow up so he can leave home and get away from his brother. He sees his friends with their siblings, all going to the same school and leading a 'normal' family life. He is happy to let Connor join in with games when he has his friends over to our house but he really hates him going anywhere near school. Things are slightly better now but up to around a year ago even picking Tom up at the school gate was a step too far for Connor. If he was ever off sick, or had a teacher training day, I had to take him with me. We would stand at the gate with me clinging on to Connor as he fought and yelled and tried to detach himself from my grip. He desperately wanted to run off into the building and cause mayhem; I obviously couldn't let him. I would stand my ground with gritted teeth, praying for Tom to appear so we could get out of there quickly. All the other parents would be staring at us, their children waiting quietly and calmly by their side.

On one occasion, at the end of term, I had been called in to collect flowers, as a thank you for my fundraising efforts. Connor had already broken up so I had to take him with me. As we were standing in reception chatting, the bell went and there was a sudden rush of pupils, all excited to get home and start their holidays. Connor had already been into most of the classrooms for a good nose round and as I didn't want him to run off again I was holding tightly on to his hand. Still waiting for Tom to appear, I carried on my conversation with the headmaster, attempting to ignore Connors' frustration levels which were rising by the second. Just as Tom appeared, followed by many of the teachers, Connor decided he'd had enough and let rip the most enormous screaming fit he could muster. He threw himself to the floor and yelled his head off, kicking out at me and hitting me with his fists. He was so angry that he wasn't allowed to run off and do what he liked. As I fought hard to control him another parent that I knew came over to help, and it took both of us to keep him from escaping. By this time we were surrounded by a crowd of children and teachers, and poor Tom was mortified. When we got home he asked me never to take Connor to his school again.

Our local health authority offered Tom a place on a sibling's course. It was to run for ten weeks and was a chance for brothers and sisters of disabled children to have some fun away from home. They did some artwork and played games and it didn't appear to be terribly exciting to me but Tom absolutely loved it. They were encouraged to talk about their feelings towards their sibling, were free to say whatever they wanted with no repercussions, and without fear of upsetting anyone. They said that many of the children were reluctant to voice their real thoughts to a member of the family, as they didn't want to cause any more distress to already struggling parents. I never got to hear what Tom said about Connor, that was the whole point of the exercise, but he came home ecstatic that he had met other children in the same boat as himself. He said that at last he didn't feel so alone.

\* \* \*

Years ago, when Connor had outgrown his push chair and ran away all the time, I was crying out for help. I hated taking him out as he was so badly behaved, but couldn't lock us all away in the house forever. I was fed up trying to cope alone all the time and called in his social workers for some support. I asked if they had people who could come out on trips with me and teach me the best way to gain some control over him. They were more experienced in dealing with children who had autism than I was, and I was sure they could help. I got a lot of sympathy but no practical assistance was available. Instead they offered a 'major buggy' which is an over sized baby stroller for bigger children. They suggested that if I couldn't cope with his running then he could be restrained in one of these. I was tempted for a split second, then realised that this wasn't the answer. He had no physical difficulties, in fact he needed the exercise more than ever; his problems were in his head, not in his legs.

We got a similar response when we were desperate to get him out of nappies. I had no idea where to start and dreaded the thought of him making a mess all over the house. I felt ill equipped to deal with this and thought I should call in the experts for guidance. Again we got a response that we didn't feel was right for him. I was told that lots of autistic children find toilets very scary and refuse to go near them. As he was now far too big for a babies' potty, we were offered a commode. I was horrified. These are meant for use by the old, fragile and immobile. Not for a very energetic, lively seven year old. It was suggested that we try it in the living room then eventually move it to the bathroom. Envisaging him doing his business in front of us all, I refused point blank. It was going to be the toilet behind closed doors, whether he liked it or not.

Coping with Connors' behaviour and attempting to understand his needs is a constant and ongoing battle. It is exhausting, and just when you feel progress has been made something happens that puts you right back at square one. Inevitably I get bad tempered and irritable at times, and I have to try not to take my frustrations out on those around me. The amount of time and effort needed just for him leaves little left for anyone else, but we all need to have a life too. Tom needs to enjoy being a kid and not be forced into the role of carer for his little brother. Frank and I need to remember that we were a couple before we had the boys, and not get swamped by the enormous complexities of parenthood. It is a delicate balancing act, and this balance needs to be restored.

# 16

## WALK WITH THE ANIMALS

For centuries animals have been used to help humans in so many areas of our lives. From horses that pull carts, leeches that help alleviate skin conditions, to dogs that act as eyes for the blind; they all play their part in some way. I loved having pets growing up, it was comforting to stroke them, and have someone you could tell all your problems to. Someone who would never comment, judge, or tell your secrets to others. Dogs especially are known for being taken to visit the sick and elderly as 'Pet's for Therapy'. I have also heard stories of various animals being used to bring autistic children back from their world in to ours. I am thrilled for those that have been helped in this way, but remain sceptical as to whether such treatments could work on Connor. But sometimes, in desperation, it is worth trying almost anything in the hope that what may not work for one, just might work for another. I would never criticise or condemn any methods available, and would love to tell you that our dog has worked wonders with him. I would love to tell you that he chats to her or has 'recovered' in some other way, but sadly that wouldn't be true. But she has helped us in so many ways and having her is great fun for us all. She is a wonderful diversion for Tom, and is always up for a tug of war or a good chase round the kitchen table. Granted it took Connor two years to become completely relaxed with her, but he got there in the end.

To show how much he considers Toffee a part of the family, he brought her a chocolate bar back from a school trip. They had, very bravely, taken his whole class down south to visit the Cadbury's factory in Birmingham. At the end of the day they were allowed to buy something from the shop, but Connor insisted on buying three things. One, he said, was for him, one was for Tom, and the third was for Toffee. The fact that she isn't allowed to eat chocolate made for humans would never occur to him, but it proved that he classes her as an equal, and that she is accepted as a family member. Although he bought her something she couldn't have, it also proves that it really is the 'thought that counts'.

Getting Toffee has also made us all get out of the house and go for walks. Even on days when the weather is bad, or days when you feel lazy or really just can't be arsed, you still have to go, regardless. We try to walk her mainly in the daytime whilst the boys are at school, but the weekends and holidays are more difficult, especially when Frank is away travelling. My parents often come over to help when I am on my own, but sometimes even all of us put together haven't been enough to control Connor.

The main issue is that he will only agree to go for a walk if you go to the places he likes the best. He loves running along beaches, or going to a large park / common that is near our home but that is as far as it goes. Try to go anywhere else and all hell breaks loose.

We live close to an old railway line that was turned into a path years ago for walking, jogging, cycling and horse riding. It is great for walking the dog as it stretches for miles, is very well maintained by the local council, and is reasonably straight so you don't lose sight of her very often. Connor however, decided long ago that it was far too boring and predictable and he dug his heels in, literally. I have attempted on numerous occasions in the past to persuade him, especially when it had rained and the thought of either a soggy beach or muddy park didn't appeal, but my efforts were met with a brick wall. Determined to at least try, I used to drag him along, kicking and screaming, for twenty yards or so, then let go and get my breath back. He would either curl up on the ground or try to turn back, but I would pick him up and carry on, over and over again, in the vain hope that he would eventually realise he wasn't going to get his own way. After half an hour of yelling I was so exhausted I would give in and turn round. The second we did this the tears dried up and he skipped happily all the way back to the car. Poor Tom was distraught as we often bumped into families from his school and they all got to witness the chaos. I even tried taking his scooter to see if that helped, but just ended up having to carry that as well as Connor. I arrived back at the car shattered and with a splitting headache, wondering yet again, why he felt the need to act like that. He did the same thing every time, even starting to yell before we got there, until I finally gave in and gave up.

Connor is an extremely determined child when he either wants, or doesn't want, to do something. There is no negotiation and zero tolerance when his mind is made up. I have fought against this rigidity for years, hoping I could wear him down and break through his resilience, but as yet he still wins.

After one of our particularly stressful attempts at a walk one day, we decided to go for an ice cream before heading home. As Tom, Connor and I sat outside the café enjoying our cones in the sun, the dog was staring from one to the other in the hope that someone was willing to share. She had eaten hers already, gulping it down in one go as she always does, not even pausing to enjoy the taste. Connor was about half way through his when he leaned over towards her. He held out his ice cream and as she took a big lick the other customers gave a loud 'aahhh'. They were touched by the fact that this caring little boy loved his dog so much that he was prepared to give up his precious treat. Surprised, but assuming that for once he had indeed had enough, I just smiled and watched with everyone else. Unfortunately though, a few licks later, Connor decided that it was actually far too tempting to give away and so moving back from the dog he carried on eating it himself. All the 'aahhh's' were immediately replaced with 'OH MY GOD!' as Connor licked away happily, completely oblivious to what he had done. The very thought of where the dog's tongue might have been minutes before didn't even enter his head, but it was clearly vivid in the minds of the rest of us.

\* \* \*

Deciding it was best to only go where he wanted, at least for the time being, we stick to the beach or park. He prefers one particular beach where he knows there is an ice cream shop before you reach the sand. He insists on getting one before he is willing to walk, but it's worth it to keep the peace. It is reasonably easy to keep an eye on him here, but it is a massive beach and rather than stroll along it he loves to head straight out to sea. Once the ice cream is safely stored away in his stomach, and his energy levels replenished, it is time to run. We always check the tide tables to ensure that the water is sufficiently far enough out for us to reach the first island, and we just let him go. He is in heaven, running free with the wind in his hair, the dog at his heels and no one yelling at him to stop. We are happy, as he is safe, in sight at all times, and can't really cause much damage apart from stopping to pull his pants down for a wee now and then. We tend to walk at a good pace so as not to be too far behind and Toffee does her best to keep up, diverting off at intervals to chase a seagull or two. His aim is to reach the small island that is a mile and a half from shore, and has been devastated on the rare occasions when I have got it wrong and the tide was in. He isn't fussy though if he gets his feet wet, as we found out on a cold afternoon a few years ago.

We arrived at the beach to find that the tide, although out, had obviously only just gone, leaving behind a beach full of puddles. These weren't small puddles though; ones that you could just step over or skip around. They were more like huge ponds that you had to wade into, and apparently, as we found out, they were deep too. Not being fazed by this at all Connor went happily on his way towards the island, and we had no choice but to follow. In an attempt to avoid the worst ones we tried to persuade him to go along to the right as opposed to straight out, but this was met with screams of defiance and he just carried on. In his mind the only reason to come here is to make it out to the island, even if he has to swim to get there. Nothing and no one can deter him from his goal. My Mum, Dad and I slowly picked our way through the pools, trying to avoid any suspicious looking yellowish ones, which may have already been visited by a dog or two. In an attempt to miss the deepest puddles my Dad and I veered off to the left while Mum decided to follow in Connors' footsteps, and as it turned out she was right. Apart from getting his trousers wet, my Dad didn't fare too badly due to his waterproof walking boots. I, on the other hand, had stupidly gone out in trainers, which let in every drop of water I stepped in. By the time we reached dry land my feet were squelching in my shoes and freezing cold. Connor, also in trainers, was soaked through too but as he doesn't really feel the cold he didn't give a toss. He ripped off his soggy socks, flung them in my direction, and sat down to play in the sand.

Before leaving the house he had picked up a few sticks from the pile that I had brought home from a recent park visit. We all thought it was lovely that he had been good enough to consider Toffee, and had brought them for her to play with. It quickly became apparent though that he had actually taken them for himself. He set to work using the sticks to dig out tunnels under the sand, and then lay down to see if he could see right through them to the other side. Poor Toffee sat watching him, hoping that eventually he would take pity on her and throw a stick for her to chase. She didn't once try to steal them though, just sat close by with a sad look on her face. Eventually, after an hour or so when the game had started to lose its appeal, and the sticks had snapped into numerous pieces, she was allowed to have them. Not being great at throwing they only landed a few paces away and she looked at him as if to say "is that it?" After nearly two hours of tunnel digging and decorating sand castles with shells, bits of old seaweed and whatever else we could find, he agreed to set off for home. We were all freezing by then and were more than ready to leave, not looking forward to another wade through the wet to reach the road. But we were excited by the fact that he had actually lasted so long and had played contentedly for once without running off. This was the first time in his whole life he had actually shown any interest in building sand castles, and we hadn't had to take turns in chasing him around the beach. It had only taken us eight long years to see it, but it was worth every second of that waiting. I drove us all home with wet socks, sore blisters, and a huge smile across my face. This was a massive achievement for us, to enjoy an afternoon out at the seaside without confrontation, tantrums and stress. I finally knew what it felt like to be a normal, typical family, and it gave me hope of brighter times to come.

* * *

His other favourite place to go is the park, and again this has the added benefit of an ice cream van situated at the entrance. He refuses to budge an inch before getting his double vanilla cone with strawberry sauce, but once satisfied is normally willing to leg around for an hour or two with the dog. There are some occasions though when he decides that he just isn't in the mood, and no amount of persuasion is going to make him co-operate. We have no clue what triggers these outbursts, and no idea how to prevent them. He will get in the car quite happily and we tell him where we are going. You don't know whether it will be a good or bad day until you get there and open the car door. He either jumps out excitedly or refuses to move, it is then that you know you are in for a fight.

One time, when he was around four or five, my Mum and Dad had come over for a walk. We didn't have the dog then, but had decided to make the most of a rare sunny day and take the boys out for some fresh air. I think we had started off the walk quite well but for some unknown reason he became more and more agitated, and after about half an hour he threw himself down on the grass. We managed to persuade him to get up, with the promise that we would head back to the car but as the paths go off in all directions we didn't literally turn around and go back exactly the same way. This seemed to irritate him immensely and as we picked our way through the trees he started screaming and curling himself up on the ground. Obviously needing to keep him mobile, I kept dragging him to his feet and pulled him along as far as I could manage until he was kicking and fighting so much I had to let go. We carried on like this for quite some time, with me, and him, getting more and more exhausted and bad tempered. Eventually, so distracted by all the commotion, we realised we were completely lost and were just going round in circles. All the paths looked similar, and as I inherited my terrible sense of direction from my Mum, none of us knew which way to go. We were now taking it in turns to half drag, half carry, Connor and he got very heavy after a while. At one point I flung him onto some long grass, with tears of frustration stinging my eyes. I was fed up having to battle with him, and was angry that we couldn't even go for a nice, enjoyable walk on a warm afternoon like all the other families there that day. After suffering the humiliation of having to ask someone for directions, we made it back to the car park. The second he was home the tears dried up and he was happy. Back in his comfort zone, the tantrum was instantly forgotten. It took my parents and I a while to pluck up the courage to venture out with him again.

Years later, not long after getting Toffee, we were subjected to another, equally stressful trip out in the same place. Again he seemed happy enough until he had devoured his ice cream, then his mood just altered for no apparent reason. As he was older now we tried to get him to tell us what was wrong, but he just yelled and kept turning back in the direction of the car. We hadn't been there long and as Toffee was bouncing around in need of more exercise we tried to carry on, but Connor was determined to go off down a different path to the one we had chosen. He ignored our pleas for him to come back, so having no alternative but to follow we ran after him, trying to catch up. Turning a corner we found him wading through a massive mud bath with the dog happily splashing around with him. Not wishing us all to get rotten I told my Dad and Tom to stay behind whilst my Mum and I attempted to squeeze around the edge, clinging onto the trees so as not to fall in. We really needed to catch up with him before he made it out the other side and kept on going. Tom, of course, too impatient to wait was trying to find his way through the water using wobbly rocks as stepping-stones. Inevitably, he trod on one that was too unstable and ended up knee deep in dirt. The dog meanwhile thought this was wonderful fun and was bounding about getting blacker and smellier by the second. Eventually my Mum and I cornered him up a steep embankment of tangled bushes and managed to march him through the trees back to the path. Once Tom had been rescued we wiped off the worst of the mud and decided to call it a day. Toffee was caked in muck from head to toe and stank to high heaven; looking like a chocolate brown Labrador as opposed to the lovely, clean yellow one she had been just thirty minutes earlier. There is nothing worse than the smell of wet dog and we were forced to drive home with all the car windows wide open.

* * *

It was about four years ago in the Easter holidays when I received an unexpected phone call from a mum at Toms' school. She was taking her three children and their black Labrador out to the park, and wondered if we'd like to join them. As Frank was away and I didn't love going out with Connor on my own I jumped at the chance. Their dog Emma is a couple of years older than Toff, and they always get on well together. As they were both from the same breeder Tom likes to think of them as half sisters, so it's nice to see them running around and playing together. We met them in the car park and after a quick diversion to the ice cream van for Connor we set off. With five young children and two excited dogs it was slightly chaotic, but manageable as long as we kept a close eye on what they were up to. I think I even dared to start enjoying myself, up until the point when they all decided it would be great fun to climb a tree. This would have been fine if Connor had any sense of danger and had not kept on going past an acceptable height. As he climbed further and further up we called to the others to stop following him and come down, it was getting out of hand and we didn't fancy spending the rest of the afternoon in A&E, or having to phone for an ambulance. Tom, Amy, Billy and Sam all carefully came down and we made them stand right out of the way in case Connor slipped and fell on top of them. I tried calling him calmly so as not to shock him, but of course he completely ignored me. This was far too much fun to listen to your annoying mother telling you what to do. Jane, the other mum I was with, started getting anxious and asked me if I was worried. As he was only about fifteen feet above the ground I was apprehensive but not overly so, well not yet anyway. But he wasn't done yet. He climbed up another few feet then coming across a thick branch he stepped on to it. The other children gasped in unison, and just stared in complete silence, not quite believing what they were seeing. I assured them that he would be fine; that he never falls off anything and this was normal behaviour for Connor. Nobody looked very convinced. He stood still for a few seconds to regain his balance then let go of the tree trunk and edged out on the branch. Now he must have been nearly twenty feet up and with nothing to hold on to he held out his hands to steady himself. He resembled a tightrope walker from the circus, the only problem being that there was no safety net underneath to save him. Everyone else looked horrified, and I had to admit that I was now very concerned for his safety. The branch was getting thinner the further he went, and was starting to look like it might snap. Trying not to sound alarmed, as I didn't want to scare either Connor or the other kids, I started to shout a little louder. I positioned myself under him in the hope that if he did slip then I could at least break his fall and prevent a very nasty accident. I wasn't confident that I would be able to catch him, and knew I might get hurt in the process, but was willing to risk anything. As we all stood watching, not sure what else to do, he suddenly turned back and made it safely to the trunk. Reaching the ground he just ran off with the others, not bothered in the least that he could have fallen to his death moments earlier. Jane and I looked at each other; the relief clear on our faces, we didn't need to voice what might have happened had he lost his grip. Needless to say, we haven't been invited out for a walk again since.

* * *

A few months later during another school holiday, I took the boys to the park on my own. Connor had by now established the routine of buy ice cream, eat it as fast as you can, then run like hell towards the high rock in the centre of the common. He adores this rock; has even named it 'Adventure

244

Island', and it is the only reason he is willing to walk the dog here. He knows the way to it from either car park and from every path, I swear he could find it blindfolded if necessary. I, on the other hand, hate them climbing up it as it is slippery, even when dry, and extremely high, but there is no way on earth that he would come here and not climb.

On this particular day it had been raining so Connor and I were in our wellington boots, whilst Tom had decided to stick to his trainers. As wellies don't have a good grip on the sole I was slightly concerned about him climbing the rock, but as I didn't have a hope in hell of stopping him, I decided not to worry about it and just go with the flow. Having to run all the way there as usual, I was panting when I eventually caught them up. Tom had managed to keep up with Connor so I knew that he would keep a vague eye on him. Toffee was already soaking wet and grubby after a quick dip in a stagnant muddy pond. There were quite a few other families there already and I needed to keep a close check on Connor to make sure he didn't push past anyone on his way up.

His favourite game is to run and jump around the top of this rock and hang precariously over the side. Other parents watch in horror as he walks around far too close to the edge, and flings himself through the air over lengthy gaps. I am now so used to him that I probably appear far too complacent to most people, but if they knew him like I do they would understand. I used to stand at the bottom yelling and screaming for him to be careful, convinced that he would fall to his death at any moment but it never made any difference. He totally ignored me as he does in any situation, and it just made me look like a neurotic lunatic to everyone else. In the end I learned to give in, and leave him to it. It is best just not to look.

Just so you get the picture, this isn't a small rock at all. In fact it is the height of a typical two-storey house, so I am justified in panicking when he leans over the edge. As I was worried he might slip in his wellies, I periodically reminded him to stay away from the side and slow down. Of course, he completely ignored my requests but I felt I had to try, and didn't want the other parents there to think I was oblivious to the danger. After an hour of constantly circling the area so that I had Connor in my vision at all times, I was getting fed up and wanted to carry on with the walk. Toffee was also bored, as I had to keep her on the lead to prevent her from following the boys. I shouted for them to get down and Tom appeared, but there was still no sign of Connor. Tom went back to find him while I held on to the dog, not wishing to give her the opportunity to escape. Moments later they both showed up, Tom having to wrestle with him, as he clearly wasn't ready to go home yet. I let go of the lead so that I could get a good grip on Connor, knowing that if I missed this opportunity I might not get a second chance for some time. Just as I grabbed him Tom decided to call to Toffee from half way up the rock, and she flew off towards him before I could react and stop her. Connor was furious that he couldn't join in, and was kicking me and yelling at the top of his voice. All the other parents just stood there, amazed at all this madness that was going on right in front of them. Not one person offered to help, or even bothered to ask if I was okay. As I fought to control Connor, Toffee reached the point where Tom was, and I shouted for them to both come down quickly as I was struggling to keep my grip. We needed to get Connor far away as fast as possible so he could calm down. Tom yelled back that he was now stuck as Toffee was blocking the way. She had somehow become wedged in the narrow gap between two parts of stone and wouldn't move. Not wanting to release Connor I yelled back to Tom that he needed to free her himself, but she refused to budge an inch in any direction. There was now quite a large queue of children forming behind the dog, as they all attempted to get past. They could have easily gone round another way, but children being children, they were attracted by all the disturbance. One child even tried to climb over her, and I needed to get her out before someone got hurt. Being alone, and with no one willing to come to my rescue, I let Connor go and went to help Tom. Reaching Toffee I saw, with relief, that she wasn't actually jammed, but couldn't move forward as the space in front was too narrow. She had no way of turning round and was too scared to back out so she just stood there, shaking. Holding on to her legs I gently pulled her backwards, and with her pads slipping on the sandstone she luckily couldn't fight me. With her safely back on ground level and secured by her lead, Tom scrambled down and joined us. Now all we had to do was get Connor, as of course he had gone straight up to the top again when he had the chance. After another few minutes of calling him and being completely ignored, I was beginning to get frustrated. Tom offered to go and get him but not wanting the cycle to start all over again, I told him to stay with me. Desperately trying not to burst into tears I screamed and shouted at Connor, while everybody else there looked on in utter amazement and shock. They must have thought I was completely crazy and had lost my mind.

Deciding to try another tactic we decided to simply walk away and leave him, in the hope that this would scare him and force him to follow. Surprisingly, this actually worked and he rushed after us, not wanting to be left behind. We made it through the trees and out onto the open expanse of the common. Exhausted by now, Tom and I headed off in the direction of the car but Connor, still clearly angry with me, had other ideas. He turned and ran the opposite way, far too annoyed to comply with my pleas for him to stop. Seeing that we were chasing him he legged it down a steep bank of heather which leads on to a very busy main road. He still had some way to go to reach the road, but being in such a bad mood I wouldn't put it past him to have made it all the way there. Tom and I decided to follow and try to catch up, and as he had trainers on he was faster than I was. I shouted to Tom to keep going, and grab hold of Connor if he caught up. I gave him the green light to use any means necessary to keep hold of him until I got there. I was way behind them and struggling to stay upright, wellies were great for the rain but I was regretting having put them on now. Eventually I reached the boys who were lying on the ground in a terrible tangle; Connor was fighting and kicking, trying to escape. Having now had about as much as I could cope with for one day, I dragged him to his feet and frog marched him back up the hill. It was pretty steep, and slippery soles combined with wet heather didn't help matters. Holding Connor tightly by the back of his coat I pushed him in front of me all the way up, determined he wasn't going to escape again. He yelled all the way home and I threw him in his bedroom and slammed the door shut. Leaving him to scream, and after locking the front door to prevent a break out, I headed for the kitchen. A large glass of red wine was a must after a day like that.

* * *

I can happily report that we have made some progress with the dog walking over the past twelve months and things are very slowly moving in the right direction. We are still restricted to his favourite places, have to buy ice creams before each walk, and even resort to using McDonald's chips as a bribe for good behaviour. He still runs at full speed everywhere we go; strolling or even a fast walk, are so out of the question. He has to be allowed to climb trees, but accommodating his needs means that at least we are able to get out of the house for a few hours and everyone is happy.

Toffee is content, we all get some much-needed fresh air, and my sanity stays fairly intact.

* * *

The most frightening experience we had whilst walking the dog occurred a few months after Connor turned eight. The saddest thing was that I was too complacent; I had dared to let down my guard. I naively believed that we were way beyond this point by now, and that he would never do what he did. The events of that day will haunt me always…

It was the school half term break in late October, so the days were getting shorter and the nights were drawing in fast. My Mum had come over to watch Tom and his friend Joe, whilst I had taken Connor to the dentist in the morning. He still hates these visits so wasn't in the best of moods, coupled with the fact that he had wanted to visit a toy store on the return journey and I had said no. I didn't want to leave my Mum alone for too long, and we still had to walk the dog. I was also concerned that it might rain, and didn't want us all getting caught in a downpour. We really needed to get home, have lunch, and get back out as soon as possible.

While the rest of us had a quick bite to eat, Connor stormed around the house, stamping his feet and punching the front door to show his frustration.

251

He was livid that he hadn't been allowed to buy yet another toy to add to the already huge collection in his bedroom. We locked the door, just to be safe, and ignored his outburst, expecting it to stop, eventually. By the time we were all ready to go he was still pretty angry, and showed little sign of calming down. Deciding it was best to leave him at home in this state, I told the boys to get in the car and we would go without him. My Mum was to be left behind to hold the fort. Just as we were all piling outside, Connor appeared in the hall. I asked him, yet again, if he wanted to come with us, expecting a loud "NO" as had been the case for the last hour. Amazingly, he calmly said "yes" and proceeded to go off in search of his shoes and jacket. Pleased at his sudden, yet very unexpected, change of heart, I locked up and drove us all the few miles to the park. After the obligatory visit to the ice cream van, the boys ran off in the direction of the dreaded rock, and my Mum and I trailed slowly behind. As they all jogged happily ahead, with Toffee bouncing around them, Connor appeared to be relaxed and calm, the tantrum seemingly forgotten. They spent the next hour climbing and running around, while my Mum and I watched from below. Once they'd all had enough, we made our way through the trees and out onto the common. As the ground here is still very rocky and uneven, we lagged behind while the boys raced off ahead in search of the tree they liked to climb. We caught up to find them clambering about in the branches, with Toffee on guard duty beneath. After another twenty minutes or so, I called for them all to come down so we could proceed with our journey. It was around 3.20pm by then, and the light was already beginning to fade. I knew that in another hour it would be getting dark, and as the car park barrier was locked at dusk, I didn't want to take any chances. Connor was a little reluctant to obey, but after a bit of persuasion and the bribe of McDonald's chips, he relented. Carrying on in the direction of the car he did the usual procedure of rushing off now and then to run up and down the odd hill or climb a small rock, but this was normal behaviour, and I didn't see any reason to worry. At one point he ran off into some trees and flatly refused to come back. Shouting him had no effect, so I sent Tom to try and get him back as he had gone quite far away from us, and was only just in sight. When neither of them returned, I decided I'd better follow. Connor was quite annoyed when I grabbed him and marched him back to join the others. For some reason he really wanted to go off in a different direction and was angry at being prevented from doing so. Back on the right path, assuming the drama was over, I let him race on ahead. He was only ten to fifteen yards in front, and could clearly be seen by the rest of us. Minutes later the boys came across another set of rocks they wanted to climb, but they were a little steep for my Mum to manage. Knowing there was an easier path literally ten feet away I said that was fine and that we'd meet them round the next bend. They must only have been out of sight for twenty to thirty seconds at most, but that proved to be enough. It gave Connor the opportunity he needed to escape, and go in the direction he wanted. I turned the corner and made my way over to the boys, expecting to see them all playing happily. Tom and Joe were there, with Toffee sniffing about in the heather, but Connor was nowhere to be seen. I wasn't the least bit bothered at this stage; I knew he'd be somewhere very close by, probably just round the next bend, or up the next path. The boys were sure that he hadn't followed them up the stone, but had no idea where he had gone. I assured them that it was fine, and that it hadn't been their responsibility to watch him, we'd find him within seconds for sure. I climbed up higher to get a good view of the immediate area, and could see quite far in every direction from where I was standing, but there was no sign of Connor anywhere. I was baffled, but still not too worried. He must be around here somewhere, maybe hiding in some bushes or behind a tree; he can't possibly have gotten far in such a short space of time. We quickly hunted around the surrounding paths, not wanting to venture too far in case Connor appeared and was unable to locate us. Extending our search we ran further afield; going round in circles; ending up back where we'd started. I was still reluctant to go further in case he found his way back, but the panic was beginning to set in. Ten minutes had elapsed by now and I fought hard not to show my fear to the boys. I was in the lead, with everyone racing behind, but none of us really knew what to do. We stopped to regroup and get our breath back for a moment. I emphasised the importance of us all staying together. I was the only one with a mobile phone, so we daren't split up in case we lost contact with each other. One lost member of the group was bad enough. As we ran on, shouting Connors name as we went, we came across some walkers. They said they'd been in the area for at least ten minutes and hadn't seen anyone; obviously we were hunting in the wrong place. I thanked them for their help and legged off up a different path. I could feel the desperation welling up inside, and the tears close to surfacing. Twenty minutes had gone by now, with no sight or sound of Connor. Panic had truly set in. Picking up the pace we started to shout louder. Tom was close behind me, with Joe and my Mum a little way back. Toffee seemed to sense something was wrong and was sticking to me like glue; I had to be careful not to trip over her as I ran. Stopping again to get our breath back Tom turned to me with tears in his eyes. He wanted reassurance that everything would be alright, and that we'd find Connor safe and well. I bent down and looked him straight in the eye, promising that Connor was fine and that without doubt we'd find him very soon. I was struggling to believe that myself by now, but had to stay strong and positive. Breaking down wasn't going to help anyone, or bring Connor back. I couldn't let Tom see how concerned I really was. My Mum caught up and suggested that we head back to the car, maybe he had gone there when he realised he was lost. As we ran on I started to contemplate the possibility of having to call the police and report him missing. It was getting late now, and would be dark very soon; we didn't have a hope in hell of finding him in the pitch black. They would have to send the helicopter up with its searchlight to track him. I could just imagine the next days' headline "incompetent mother loses disabled son in the woods", social services would have a field day. Nearing the car we stumbled across a family who had heard us shouting Connors' name. They said a young boy had passed them minutes before and when they asked him his name he just said "granny" then legged off again. Sensing there was something wrong, the Mum had chased after him. Thanking them profusely, we headed off in the direction they described. Desperate to catch her up, I ran as fast as I could. We were pretty tired by now as thirty minutes had elapsed since he disappeared, but sheer adrenalin kept us going. I soon spotted the lady up ahead and saw that she had stopped. As I caught up she said she had followed Connor up to that point, but had no idea which way he'd gone now. Telling her to go back to her family, I yelled to Tom to retrace his steps and find my mum and Joe. No one else was in sight now, and they needed to stay together. Toffee and I would go it alone from here. There were five paths to choose from and I had a split second to decide which one to go down. Realising I was heading roughly in the direction of the big rock, his favourite place, for once I guessed correctly. As I sped along, with the dog at my heels, I imagined the horror people must feel when they lose a child. I had lost him before, on countless occasions, but never for any length of time, and never in a place where he would be so vulnerable. I couldn't believe how quickly he had managed to disappear, to vanish completely out of sight in seconds. I think he really didn't intend to lose us, but probably assumed that we would be following close behind. I wondered how he must have felt when he saw we weren't there. I envisaged him frightened and alone, and wondered what was going through his head. All that mattered at that moment in time was finding Connor, nothing else was important. I was struggling to breathe, never having been a good long distance runner, but determination and fear kept me going. I had to find him at any cost, and would have fought through anything or anyone who got in my way. As I neared the rock the emotion in my voice was clearly apparent. I was screaming his name as loud as I could, desperate to hear any answer. As I paused for breath I heard a little voice in the distance calling out "MUMMY". It sounded like Connor but I wasn't too sure as there were other families around the area. Looking frantically about I still couldn't see him, but I kept on yelling his name. Just then he stood up and started making his way towards me, he must have been so scared that he had hidden in the bushes, unsure what else to do. As we met in the middle, with arms outstretched, we hugged each other tightly. He was visibly shaken, and very pleased to see me. I was unable to utter a single word; the tears of relief streaming down my face. Connor took a step back and whispered "mummy it's time to go home". I smiled through the tears, agreeing with him wholeheartedly. Never had I been so relieved to reach the sanctuary of home.

It was hours later, when I was finally alone, that I allowed myself to dwell on the events of the day. The very thought of what may have happened if someone with unsavoury intentions had found him first, didn't bear contemplating. He could also have fallen and badly injured himself, or drowned in one of the many ponds around the common. We'll never know what he was doing, or how he was feeling during those lost thirty minutes, and we'll never know why he decided to run.

It took me a good while to recover from the shock of that afternoon, but at least we had a happy outcome in the end. I felt compelled to write to a local newspaper to thank the lady and her family. Without their help it might have taken much longer to locate him, and I didn't want their good deed to go unnoticed. Most people are scared to get involved these days; we are just lucky that they were there, and had the common sense to realise something was amiss.

I hope Connor learnt his lesson that day, but I fear not. Now that the incident is forgotten, I wouldn't put it past him to try it again. I now know that it still isn't safe to take my eyes off him when out of the house, and that letting him wear a black coat on a dark afternoon isn't a good idea either. It is too hard to spot him darting between the trees dressed like that, and he now has a bright yellow fluorescent jacket to wear in such conditions. I even had a dog tag engraved with my mobile number to attach to his clothes, with the words 'I AM AUTISTIC' on the other side. Whether anyone would notice it I don't know, but I felt it was worth a try. I looked into getting tailor made wrist bands or other such devices, but he would go berserk and refuse to wear them, or rip them off.

Connor could still never tell anyone where he lived, who he was out with, what his phone number was, or recall the colour of our car. He knows his name, but may not answer appropriately when asked a question. He remains as vulnerable and naive as two year old, and therefore needs that high level of protection. I just have to ensure that I never lose him again.

# 17

## A THIN LINE BETWEEN LOVE AND

## HATE

Many of us have a love / hate relationship with lots of the things we come across in our everyday lives. Some people hate heights, enclosed spaces or the sight of blood. Others may have a fear of flying, or detest all things creepy and crawly. On the flip side, there are those of us who like nothing better than scaring ourselves to death. Participating in dangerous sporting activities, or going on stomach churning fair-ground rides are a great thrill for the brave. I happen to love raw onions, marmite, sad movies and soppy love songs. Frank hates them all.

So far I have been quite lucky in my life, as most things don't seem to scare me too much. I steer clear of those things I really dislike and tolerate those that are manageable. I love swimming, but hate to put my head under; a rather unfortunate scuba diving experience years ago didn't do much to help. Whenever a spider or other equally uninvited creature descends on our house it is always me who has to get rid of it. Not because I particularly like them, but no one else is willing to do it. I will still yell like a baby if they so much as start to crawl up the brush handle towards my hand, or take flight unexpectedly, but will persevere until the unwanted guest is safely deposited far into the garden, in the hope that it won't find its way back in. I have never adored plane journeys, but accept that they are a necessary part of my life if I want to travel anywhere remotely exotic, and after spending twenty four hours on a ferry with my head down the toilet, I'm not so keen on boats either.

At Toms' school summer fair one year, I had an eight-foot python draped around my shoulders. It wasn't the least bit scary and was actually quite nice to stroke, but it did get rather heavy after ten to fifteen minutes. Not everybody's cup of tea I know, but I was quite proud of myself for doing it. I jumped out of my skin when a bird flew down the chimney into my office at home recently, I don't think I've ever moved so fast, and I did scream in Spain one summer when I turned around in the shower and discovered I was not alone. Sadly it wasn't Frank who had sneaked quietly in behind me; it was a rather large scary looking insect. Even as a nature lover, I have to draw the line at sharing my shower cubicle with a three inch long flying bug.

But even when scared, I am able to rationalise those fears. Although I think spiders are creepy, I know most of them can't harm me. I knew that python wouldn't do any damage as long as it didn't feel threatened, and even when the bird flew straight at me, its wings flapping wildly around my head, I knew it was only trying to escape. I have the ability to understand the difference between situations that are genuinely life threatening, and those that just appear to be. For a person with autism though, many things in this world can appear very intimidating indeed. It must be extremely difficult to make sense of a world you don't understand. With heightened senses, a place that is noisy, bright, or has crowds of people bustling past must be sensory overload, especially to someone with limited or no speech, or for those who find communicating difficult. Maybe that explains why Connors' behaviour patterns can alter so dramatically from one place to another or from one day to the next. We have endured dozens of horrendous temper tantrums, escape attempts and lie down protests in the past, mainly when out of the house. Airports, shops and open spaces seem to be the places that can bring out the worst in Connor. If he gets his own way then he is normally quite calm, but sadly in this life that is rarely feasible. He looks like a spoilt brat when he acts badly and it can get quite embarrassing for those who are with him. It is a sad reflection on society when Tom refuses to be seen in public with his own brother. He has yet to learn the art of being thick skinned and ignoring the comments and stares from strangers. It breaks my heart that Connor is not welcome at his own brothers' birthday parties, but we don't blame Tom one bit, and fully understand his reasons. It just doesn't seem fair that they are both missing out on this brotherly bond they should be forming while they are young.

Connors' love / hate relationships with things extend into most areas of his life. Those he loves he does so with excitement, exuberance and passion. I would go so far as saying that he is obsessed over some things such as running, climbing and jumping. He has to run, even around the house, walking is just not an option. He will jump two or three stairs at a time, either going up or down, and can often be found perched on top of the post at the bottom of the staircase. He can balance on this expertly, feet together, knees bent, with arms outstretched and hands in the air. It used to scare me to death when I found him walking around the top of the banisters upstairs, with the long drop below. One slight slip or lapse of concentration would have had catastrophic results, but his grip never faltered, and he never once fell. No amount of pleading could get him to stop, and he had no idea how dangerous it was. Knowing he was being careful did nothing to calm the nerves. I even called in his care workers and the occupational therapist, desperate to find ways to protect him, but short of boarding up the whole house and turning the place into a prison, there was little we could do. Not being prepared to put the rest of us through that we declined their offer, praying instead that he would grow out of his acrobatic phase one day. We are still waiting, and he shows no signs of calming down yet.

The running is compulsory wherever he goes and is something he is very good at. He can move with lightning speed, and rarely seems to run out of steam. He never gets out of breath and can keep going for hours at a time, making things very difficult when the rest of us collapse with exhaustion. Waiting is just far too slow in Connors' opinion; a complete waste of precious time that could be better spent doing something much more fun.

* * *

He adores bouncing, on anything and everything he can find. The trampoline must certainly be the best value for money item we have ever invested in. Luckily, we have a large conservatory at the bottom of the garden to keep it in, so it can be used all year round, regardless of the weather. Connors' first priority when he gets home from school is a good long bounce, pausing on the way for a drink of course. He will rush across the patio in bare feet, not caring a toss if it's hot, cold, wet, icy or even thick snow. Nothing and no one can deter him from his favourite activity. If he didn't use up his energy this way I hate to think what he would be like. He would stay out there all night given half a chance, never getting tired or bored. I even think the repetitive movements might be a comfort to him in some way. When he was younger he loved to dash from one side of a room to the other, over and over again, as though the familiarity, rather than the exercise itself, was what he craved.

* * *

He also adores to swim, and has become very competent at this now. This makes summer holidays much less stressful, as we don't have to panic every time he ventures near the side of the pool. By copying Tom he has learnt to dive down with a mask, summersault under water, and retrieve items from the bottom of the pool. I used to take him to a private session at a public baths at the weekends. Of course he would disobey every rule, would race round and round the edge, slipping on the wet surface, and try to wee into the water. You had to watch him like a hawk and take turns in chasing after him, but we were responsible for our own party so there were no staff on hand to complain. I still haven't plucked up the courage to go to a public session with him yet for fear of what he might do.

His sister Jayne bravely took him once to the baths with Tom; confident that he would behave for her and do everything he was told. She returned home exhausted, reporting that he had been chased round the edge of the pool by her and the lifeguards, and it had taken them quite some time to catch him. As this is so dangerous and is strictly forbidden, they had been forced to leave early under a cloud of shame. She never did offer to take him swimming again.

* * *

He loves TV programmes and films, and we often find every TV set on in the house with something different playing on each one. He will flit from room to room watching bits of each programme, and is not amused if you turn over or

267

switch one off. Connor is excellent at multi tasking and can watch a movie, draw a picture, surf the internet, eat toast and play with a toy all at the same time. He has an enormous collection of DVD's, strewn all over his bedroom floor, but can always find the one he wants with lightning speed. He is not very careful with them though, and many of them jump as they are so battered and scratched. It has cost us a fortune having to re-buy the ones Tom likes the most, and these new versions have to be closely monitored so they don't fall into Connors' clutches.

He really struggles hard to contain himself if someone else tries to take possession of the remote control. He hates not being able to rewind a programme and watch his favourite part over and over again. He will watch a particular scene countless times, finding it equally as funny each time. This does get rather wearing, especially for Tom if he is trying to watch something with Connor and it gets constantly rewound. Having to view things with no sound, in fast-forward, or in reverse becomes equally frustrating after a while.

\* \* \*

He has a passion for dancing and listening to music, but refuses to dance at his school discos. The small collection of his favourite songs, have to be played time and time again, and he listens intently without uttering a single sound. It does get a bit tedious on a long car journey when you are subjected to the same track repeatedly all the way there. He will play a song thirty times in a row, never tiring of hearing the same words, though he never sings along. Days later he will spontaneously burst out into song, and we get at least two verses and the chorus. The words, tune and pitch are perfect; he even mimics the voice of the singer.

One of Toms' classmates got more than she bargained for one day. We were all waiting for the Judo after school club to finish when Connor turned to face her, threw his arms high in the air, and sang the first few lines of a love song at the top of his voice. The poor girl didn't know what to think, and everyone else stood in stunned silence. He was standing so close I had visions of him either hugging, or worse still kissing her. I moved him away quickly, before he had the chance to get any ideas.

One particular moment that touched me so deeply happened years ago, when he was younger, didn't communicate well, and was much harder to handle. It was during the school holidays, which were always stressful, and he had been very badly behaved all day. By the evening I was tired, emotional and my patience was wearing extremely thin. I agreed that the boys could stay up late to watch a movie, so we dimmed the lights and all settled on the sofa, with me at one end, Tom at the other, and Connor snuggled up in the middle. They had chosen to see the Disney film 'Space Jam', which opens with the R. Kelly song 'I Believe I Can Fly'. We watched the adverts, then there were a few moments of silence while the opening credits rolled. As we all sat waiting for the music to begin, Connor suddenly jumped up. Out of the darkness came this beautiful, clear, little voice, singing quietly, breaking the silence. Tom and I sat bolt upright and stared, open mouthed, at Connor. I had never heard him sing the words of a real song before; had no clue that he could even learn the lyrics and repeat them so perfectly. All the frustrations of the day disappeared in an instant, and as I hugged him tightly to me the tears poured down my face. Tom couldn't understand what all the fuss was about, so what he sang, big deal. But to me this was major progress; this was huge. This was a voice we thought we might never get to hear. A child we once feared might never be able to learn the most basic of things. The fact that he had memorised words and repeated them so well, gave us the hope we'd been waiting for.

Not long after starting school a teacher had said something to me that I hadn't forgotten. He had said that despite all of Connors' problems he believed that he was extremely intelligent; we just needed to find a way of reaching inside his mind. He felt that if we could find the key to unlock the door, he would simply fly. That comment made the words of the song so much more significant. Connor, of course, had no idea what those words meant, but they warmed my heart so deeply.

* * *

Other things Connor loves to do to pass the time are reading, drawing and colouring, computer games and playing with his toys. He is often found engrossed in a book or magazine, and has done this from a very early age. He can read quite well now, but when exactly he learnt this skill we are unsure. He adores drawing his favourite characters, printing them off the Internet to colour in, or get you to draw them for him. He will thrust a picture in front of us and expect it to be copied perfectly, down to the finest detail, even leaning over your shoulder whilst you draw and pointing out any bits missed. He is extremely particular, and if you dare to give him a less than perfect picture it gets screwed up in disgust and thrown in the nearest bin.

He loves playing games on his Sony Play Station, or Nintendo DS consoles. He asks Tom for help if he gets stuck, knowing full well that I am no use when it comes to things like that, Brain Training being the only game I can manage. He has taught himself how to play most of them, being able to pick up on things remarkably quickly, and yells at the screen if the characters don't do exactly what he wants them to.

He still enjoys playing with toys that he has had from an early age, never seeming to grow out of them and move on. He doesn't get angry now when I tidy up or move his things, but eventually they all seem to drift back out of the toy boxes and are reinstated into their rightful place. At times we haven't been able to move in his bedroom for all the cars, trucks and planes laid out on the floor in neat, perfect rows. He also adores Lego and wooden blocks, and will spend hours constructing vehicles or buildings.

One day, he had laid out a mat with pictures of roads on, and had built a whole town on top of it. Cars, lorries and trucks were strategically placed, together with Lego houses and garages made from wooden bricks. Each garage was sized specifically for the vehicle that was to go inside, and he was very proud of his creation. My Mum and I were sitting in the room with Connor, watching him play, when Toffee wandered in for a nose around. She expertly picked her way through the maze, careful not to place a paw on any of the objects. Things were going fine until I made the fatal mistake of speaking to her, which inevitably set off her tail wagging at full speed. As she weaved her way towards me, still being careful not to stand on anything, her thick heavy tail swung wildly from side to side. I guided her closer to the door, but just as she was nearly clear a tall garage housing numerous cars came crashing down to earth, with bricks flying in every direction. Connor was not amused. Before the crying could intensify, we shoved the dog out of the room and rebuilt the structure as best we could. She had tried so hard not to mess anything up, but her tail had let her down.

* * *

Connor still really struggles with the art of waiting. Having to wait in a queue is getting slightly easier, though if it is for more than a few minutes then it becomes a real problem. If he wants something to eat or drink he can't see why he sometimes needs to hang on for a second, and waiting his turn for the computer is still very difficult. He hates not being in control, and lives life for the moment.

His biggest fear used to be the cinema. This we felt was a terrible shame as he loved films so much, but just couldn't get over the phobia of going into the room. He talked incessantly about new movies being released, but when I dared to mention the dreaded word I got a loud "NO". As much as he wanted to see a new film, he had to wait for it to come out on DVD, as the fear of going to the pictures was far too great. This fear, I think, stemmed from his first experience many years ago.

We had met up with one of Toms' friends, his sister and their Mum Sue, outside the complex. Confident that Connor would love it, we bought our tickets and some sweets and drinks for the kids. Being early, the lights were still on when we walked in and took our seats, and as the children were still little, they wanted to sit right at the front for a better view. As the lights dimmed and the presentation started Connor looked a little shocked and reached out to hold my hand. Assuming that the darkness was scaring him I stroked his hand and whispered encouragement. The adverts started and the sound was turned up to full volume. I hoped that if we could get through the trailers then Connor would become immersed in the film and forget all about being scared. Sadly we never got that far. After a few minutes he suddenly pulled his hand away, jumped up and ran for his life out the door as fast as his legs would carry him. Worried that he might run right out into the road I chased after him, leaving everyone else behind. I caught up and led him into the ladies toilets to calm down. He was totally distraught and was fighting for breath. Unable to control his fear he just stood there shaking for about ten minutes, with one hand on the counter to steady himself. Ignoring my attempts to talk to him, he closed his eyes and repeated over and over again "calm down, what's the matter, calm down, what's the matter." I felt so sorry for him; I could see how upset he was and felt powerless to help. Eventually he agreed to leave the bathroom but it was obvious that we weren't going to be able to watch the movie. I was now faced with the dilemma of having to go back and tell the others that we had to leave, but not being able to trust Connor to wait outside on his own. I had no other choice but to drag him back down to the front row kicking and screaming to retrieve my bag and tell Sue what was going on. Leaving Tom to enjoy the film, Connor and I spent the next two hours traipsing round the nearest supermarket until they came out.

Years later we tried again but didn't even make it past the front door that time. I feared Connor could never get over this hurdle, and would refuse to set foot in a cinema forever, but amazingly, about eight months ago, a miracle occurred. I mentioned going to see a film, fully expecting the usual yells of "NO", but he quite calmly said "yes, go to cinema". I couldn't believe what I'd heard, and kept repeating it over the next few days just to be sure, but he didn't waver and even chose a film on the Odeon website. Dragging Tom along for moral support, we set off and arrived at the complex a few miles away. He tolerated the ticket queue pretty well, and after a quick diversion for drinks and sweets we settled into our seats. Feeling rather pessimistic, I was positive we'd last no more than a couple of minutes before he yelled the place down and ran out, but I was ecstatic to be proved wrong. Apart from periodically putting his hands over his ears, and a bit of bouncing up and down in the seat, he behaved brilliantly. We sat through the whole film with him smiling and laughing throughout; even Tom was impressed at his conduct. Finally we had discovered an activity we could all take part in which didn't result in stress, conflict or tantrums.

# 18

## ESPANA

The true meaning of the word 'HOLIDAY' as defined in the Oxford English Dictionary is 'an extended period of leisure, away from home, when no work is done'. I think this must have been written by someone who was either rich enough to employ a full time nanny, or who never had children at all. Either way, I really struggle to compare this analogy to some of our past summers with Connor. They could more accurately be described as extended periods of severe trauma, extreme tests of endurance and stamina, or visits to hell and back.

It was always more stressful when Connor was off school. Weekends used to be bad enough, a whole week or two was sheer torture, but the six-week break in the summer was off the scale on the stress charts. I envy those parents at Toms' school who stand at the gate in early September and tell stories of wonderful, relaxing weeks away in the sun. They got through numerous novels whilst developing a deep golden tan, their children happily splashing around in the waves, or building sandcastles for hours on end. There would be hotel kids clubs where they could be entertained by the staff, leaving Mum and Dad free to enjoy a romantic dinner alone, in peace. The whole family would return relaxed, rejuvenated and with their batteries recharged, happy to go back to work and school with pleasant memories of their time together. I would appear at the gate looking pale, tired and totally wiped out. If anyone was brave enough to ask how my summer went they were met with a twenty- minute rendition of every tantrum, yelling fit and detail of how badly behaved Connor had been for the past six weeks. They looked shocked, and were relieved when I finally ran out of steam. Eventually, I realised that most people actually didn't want to hear the truth, they were only asking out of politeness. It was the obvious question when waving your children goodbye on their first day back. Now, when asked how our holidays went I just nod, smile, and say "great yes, how was yours?"

Travelling abroad with Connor these days is in fact a massive improvement on past years. He can still get agitated at the airport if the check in or customs queues are too long, and still insists on running off to hunt out any DVD stores. We are sure he is calmer now he understands exactly where he is going, as we always take him to the same place each summer. He gets fed up on the plane, as many children do, but can be kept occupied with magazines, colouring books, computer games and portable DVD player. It is extremely hard to keep him quiet though. If he is watching a cartoon that he finds particularly funny he will laugh his head off, very loudly. No amount of shushing ever works, he is in his own little world, a bubble that none of us can penetrate. He has no clue that his screaming with laughter is not something that everyone else wants to hear. Although, this is preferable to the sound of a temper tantrum, that we have had so many of in the past.

* * *

We have been taking Connor to Spain since he was around the age of two. Before we built our own house we stayed in rented villas close to where our plot was. We liked the area, and it was good to get to know our way round and keep an eye on the progress. The Spanish building company didn't seem to be in any particular hurry, and it must have taken around a year and a half to two years from choosing the plot of land to finally handing over the keys. We still faced an array of problems when it

279

was supposedly finished, but that's another story. Bearing in mind Connors' climbing abilities, and the fact that both boys were still very young, we tried to make it as safe as possible. This proved pretty difficult in a country where health and safety doesn't appear to be at the top of the list of priorities. Many houses in Spain are single storey, with the living area on one level, but we had chosen a plot up a mountain. It was therefore better to build our house the height of a two-storey building, meaning we really lived upstairs with an empty space below. This lower level could be converted into rooms in the future, if we can ever afford it! The only downside was that it meant it was a long way down if Connor decided to jump out a window, or attempt a superman style descent off the top of the pool balcony. We asked for all the windows to have a tilt option so that they could be opened enough to let the air in, but not enough for Connor to be able to climb out, but of course we were ignored and only some of them have this. We also insisted that there must be none, or at least very few, steps leading down to the pool area and all the outdoor tiles be non-slip. We now have to negotiate six reasonably steep steps and as predicted, the so-called non-slip floor is lethal when wet. We also had heated debates with the builders over the pool leaking for at least two years, and the filter developing cracks due to them installing one that was too small for the volume of water, but trying to fight the system when you can't speak their language proved virtually impossible.

* * *

One year when Connor was around two or three, we rented a house off a friend of one of the builders. The property itself had recently been renovated and was nice inside, but the pool had only been filled the day before we got there, and was freezing. The boys managed to dip their feet in but it was really too cold to swim, which seemed a shame, but this wasn't the only problem. Surrounding the villa were other vacant properties, which were in various states of being renovated, and to protect them at night they left guard dogs roaming the grounds. Each time one of the dogs barked this set off a whole chorus of high pitched deafening sounds that went on all night. After about a week Frank was ready to kill someone. I sleep deeper than him so I could shut out the noise, but he'd had more than enough. He went to the estate agents and found us a villa close to where the house was being built. He assured me that it was safe for the boys, and had been inside to make doubly sure. We packed up and moved, but when we got inside I was horrified. It was clear that no one had stayed there for quite some time and the beds, sheets and pillows were damp and mouldy. I had to wash all the dishes before we dared to use them, and there was a suspicious looking mound of god knows what, growing in one of the cupboards. But still, nothing a little bleach and washing powder couldn't fix. All that though paled into insignificance when I saw the health and safety nightmare in the living room. The bedrooms, bathroom, and pool were on the lower level and were accessed by a steep open tiled staircase leading from the middle of the upper area. There was no guardrail at the top, and nothing to hold on to on the way down. It was a potential death trap, and on top of everything else, just too much to bear. I let rip, big time. I think that was the first time Frank had witnessed me losing my temper. I just couldn't believe that having vetted the property he deemed it safe for the boys, or even habitable at all. Anyway we muddled through the next week, and thankfully arrived home with body parts intact.

* * *

While Connor was still young enough to be in a buggy, the journey through the airport was manageable. That is to say he was contained and couldn't escape, but we had no control over his yelling fits. We got through the check in by diverting his attention with drinks, food or a favourite toy. If this didn't work, or the queue was so long that we ran out of things to offer, I would take him off to the bathroom to waste some time. Next we had to negotiate the customs line. This was often very long and slow moving, but we just had to stand there and wait our turn. He would persist with the screaming and shouting, but at least we couldn't lose him.

Waiting for the flight is supposed to be an exciting part of the whole holiday experience. The kids can get hyped up on fast food additives, with Mum and Dad starting to relax, looking forward to a few weeks in the sun. We certainly had an experience, but not in a good way. The nightmare really began when he became too old to be pushed around, and had to be allowed to roam free. When the check in queues were lengthy we asked the staff for assistance, and most airlines were happy to bump us to the front of the line. We still had customs to get through though, and there was no way of bypassing that one.

We had no option but to wait and endure some of the worst screaming fits he has ever been able to muster. For some reason these airport queues brought out the worst in Connor, we have no idea why. It wasn't like in the park or at a store, where we could simply remove him from the scene and therefore diffuse the situation. We had to stand our ground and just cope as best we could. He would yell and squirm, flinging himself on the ground in an attempt to escape my grip. Equally determined I would drag him up, move forwards a few feet then allow him to drop to the floor again. He would scream as loud as he possibly could, desperate to get away from the crowds. As he disappeared off under the barrier I would kneel down and yank him back by the ankles. His face would be sopping wet from sweat and tears; mine wasn't far behind from all the exertion. Standing up straight I held my place in the line, clinging on to a writhing, angry child, staring straight ahead, careful not to catch the eye of any of the other passengers. As human nature dictates, people just couldn't help but stare at us, unable to hide their disdain at the disaster unfolding in front of them. Not one person ever offered the slightest ounce of sympathy or assistance. You could see them secretly praying that we weren't on the same flight as they were. By the time we were through to the departure lounge I was ready to call it a day and go back home, this wasn't how a relaxing holiday in the sun was supposed to start.

One year he broke free from my grip and ran off around the gate area. He wasn't really causing any trouble, but with so many people there I was afraid that we would lose him completely. Rather than causing a yelling fit by attempting to keep him still, I let him run and just chased after him as fast as I could. It was so crowded there were groups of passengers sitting all over the airport floor waiting patiently for their flights. They seemed less than amused to have a runaway little boy clambering over them, and his lunatic mother not far behind calling out his name in a futile attempt to stop the running. I decided not to look down at the faces glaring up at me as I jumped over legs and squeezed through gaps in the crowd. I wanted to stop and yell at them all "trust me this is nothing to what he'll do if I catch him and force him to stay still" but of course I never did. It was safer to let him have his fix, as he would soon be confined for the next two and a half hours, strapped into his seat on the plane.

Another year we made it through the check in and took him to choose a DVD in the store before going through customs. This was the only shop selling this type of thing, and once we had gotten through to departures there was obviously no going back. He circled the racks over and over again, but couldn't seem to find what he wanted. As we were running out of time we picked up various films to try and persuade him to choose, but he refused all

285

the ones we offered. Leaving of his own accord he wandered out, empty-handed. We bought two films that he had shown some interest in, in the hope of keeping him happy, then joined the queue at the bag scanner. Once through the barrier we wandered around and found a small play area with various arcade type machines. Breathing a sigh of relief we figured we had got off quite lightly, and settled down to watch the boys. Minutes later though, we were in for a shock. Seemingly from nowhere, Connor totally freaked out. He was screaming at full volume, running around in circles, and shaking his clenched fists in the air. Everyone around us just couldn't help but stare in utter amazement at this sudden and furious outburst. We were pretty shocked ourselves, as we had been so confident that he was happy and reasonably calm that afternoon. It took me a while to work out the cause of the anger, but eventually we figured that he had wanted a particular DVD from the store, but it wasn't one of the ones we had bought. Having now come through to the departure lounge there was no way of getting back to the shop, but nothing I tried could put and end to the yelling. I attempted to reason with him, bargain with him, cuddled him and yelled back, but the more I did, the worse he got. Not wanting to get on the plane with him in this state, Frank managed to find an airport worker that was willing to help us. One of the security staff actually went back through the barrier and purchased the sought after film on our behalf. By the time he came back the tantrum had been going on for at least thirty minutes and we were all exhausted. The second he had the box in his hands the screaming subsided, but rather than sit and cherish it, or ask for his portable player to watch it there and then, he calmly stuffed it into his backpack and carried on playing as if nothing had happened. It is so difficult to understand how he can swing from calm to madness in seconds, and then back again. His moods can swing as fast as turning a light on and off, and we have absolutely no control over them. More worryingly, we also have no warning as to when he might erupt. Some may say that we shouldn't have given in to his demands, that we had already given him the opportunity to choose what he wanted earlier, and it was tough luck. But knowing from bitter experience just what he is capable of, it was worth the money to keep the peace. No one would wish to witness one of Connors' outbursts at thirty thousand feet.

Apart from wanting to choose his own seat, and repeatedly flapping the window blinds up and down, he has been manageable in the air. There was one incident though not long ago, where we were about an hour and a half into a flight, when the woman in front of him turned to ask if I could stop him from kicking her chair. Apparently he had been doing it for the whole journey and she was, quite rightly, pretty hacked off. After apologising past myself, and severely telling Connor off, I sank back in my chair fighting back the tears that were threatening to flow. Having Tom in between us I hadn't noticed what Connor was doing, but that was no excuse. I was his mother, and therefore was responsible for his behaviour towards others. The lady had been rather stroppy towards me, but then backed down when I explained about his autism, but the damage had already been done. I was totally ashamed and embarrassed by what had happened, and rather pissed off that we couldn't even get through a few hours without some kind of issue.

When we arrive at our destination the drama is still far from over. Connor is very uncomfortable being away from home and familiarity. He doesn't appear to always require strict timetables, and can cope with some changes in routine, but still prefers to be in his own cocoon of normality. Any alterations to this can throw him off balance, and make his behaviour even more unstable and unpredictable. That's not to say that he never enjoys himself though, and he will swim with Tom for hours in the pool without any problems whatsoever. Five minutes later we might find him hammering hell out the front door demanding to go back home, tears pouring down his face. Ten minutes after that he would be happily drawing pictures of his favourite cartoon characters and stuffing down pretzels. An hour later he would be back at square one again, banging on the door to escape. I have to write down the days and tick them off until it is time to leave so he knows that he will go home eventually.

We do try to go out as much as possible when we are in Spain, but every trip with Connor has the potential of becoming very stressful, and it can be quite wearing after a while. Most days we stock up the fridge and stay by the pool, the headache of going out just too much to bear. There is a McDonalds with a big play area about twenty minutes drive away so we go there a few times to keep him happy. There is also a small park about ten minutes walk from the house where the boys like to scooter along the paths. I can normally keep control of Connor there, but going to the beach has proved to be a lot more challenging.

In the height of summer the sands are pretty crowded, which makes him harder to spot when he runs off from us. One day when we had ventured out, I managed to lose him again. Frank had gone off to find a bin for our rubbish, so I was left alone with the boys. We found an empty spot near the lifeguard and settled down to relax. It was roasting hot and we had hoped that he would play in the sand for a little while at least, but Connor had other ideas. Before Frank had even returned, he legged off from me down the beach. Not wanting us all to disappear, I told Tom to stay with our bags and wait for his Dad while I gave chase. Being quite a few years ago Tom was still young and nervous at being left alone, but I had no choice. Connor was already out of sight and if I didn't go now there was no knowing what he might get up to. I was also rather concerned about someone snatching him, rare I know, but not unheard of in some countries, and a young child wandering alone would be a perfect target for a potential kidnapper. Telling Tom to stay put by the lifeguard I rushed off down the beach. I couldn't see him anywhere and decided I better check the water first and the slippery rocks he had been climbing on half an hour before. Still not finding him I widened my search to the back of the sand where there was a little kids play area, but he didn't seem to be there either. At least ten minutes had gone by now and I was starting to get anxious. Racing towards the road and car park I saw that there was a narrow stream of water snaking inland from the sea. Right at the back of the beach this stream disappeared off under a low tunnel and I felt compelled to bend down to look inside. As I did I saw a bare foot vanishing off into the darkness and breathed a sigh of relief. Jumping down I grabbed at the foot and pulled it out with a rather angry little boy attached. Marching him back to where Frank and Tom were standing I announced that I'd had enough and we had to go. I think that was the only visit to the beach we dared try that summer.

Eating out is still, and always has been, a huge hurdle for Connor. He cannot seem to comprehend why he should sit at a table nice and quietly eating his dinner. This is made worse by the fact that there are very few foods he will actually eat, and even if he will eat something at one place he won't like the same type of food somewhere else. We have only found two restaurants we can go to in Spain, apart from McDonalds of course. One is in the town closest to our villa where we have to sit inside so he can see the screen of his DVD player. Out in the sunshine he can't see the picture and all hell breaks loose, so we are always forced to go in and miss out on a nice sunny afternoon. We are not allowed to go in however, until we have visited the cheap Chinese store next door to buy a toy. This process is a necessary part of getting him to sit and eat anything and must be adhered to every single time we go, without fail. The consequences of not doing so would be catastrophic, and extremely loud. Once satisfied with his choice of plastic plaything, he will happily sit for about an hour eating chips and laughing loudly to a favourite film. We put headphones on him to save us all from having to listen, but can't mute his mouth. It's not ideal but enables us to get out for lunch now and then.

The only other place we are allowed to visit is a Chinese restaurant within walking distance of the house. Again we have to be reasonably fast eating dinner, you are not able to sit around, relax, and take your time. There is only a small window, in which he will tolerate having to behave, and he still needs his DVD player or Nintendo DS console to divert his attention, but at least we can get out. This may not sound like a relaxing evening out, but is a great improvement on previous years. I remember when Connor was really young, still in a buggy, and we couldn't enter any restaurants with him. He was happy being pushed around in the street, but the second we tried to go through a door he would immediately start screaming until you took him back outside. We could never quite tell what triggered these explosions, but he was determined not to cross the threshold of anywhere we tried to go. We ended up having to take turns in gulping down a few mouthfuls then swapping with each other at the door. One of us had to walk up and down the street while the other had a quick bite of food before switching again. It was a ridiculous way to have to manage our evening meal, and after a few occasions like this we decided it just wasn't worth trying to go out at all.

Apart from not getting out much, he is reasonably manageable at the villa as long as he has access to the swimming pool, his DVD player, games console, toys, books and plenty of pens and paper. He loves to spend hours each day drawing and colouring pictures, and as this is one of his safer activities we are more than happy to oblige. He does protest however, when any uninvited guests invade his privacy, that is completely unacceptable to him. By 'guests' I mean any living creature that is not of the human sort, and in Spain the bugs are excessively large compared to those in the UK.

He rushed in off the balcony one day in hysterics shouting "BUZZ FLY" at the top of his voice. Expecting to find something huge and scary I went out to investigate, but at first couldn't see anything at all. Assuming it had maybe flown off I went to go back in, but Connor was still yelling and pointing to the floor. Turning back I bent down and peered around the edge of the wall, eventually I spotted something that resembled a ball of dried up mud and gave it a little nudge with my finger. It slowly uncurled itself, and turned out to be a tiny, beautifully patterned, lizard. Depositing it safely into the garden, I went back in to find Connor frantically finishing off his third picture of this massive monster, surrounded by a whole array of weapons.

I have to admit though, he does have a point, and even though I am fascinated by nature and prefer not to harm anything if at all possible, some of the bugs that fly in are pretty enormous. There are ones that are inches long and resemble elongated, thin wasps with wide-open wings. Others are like big fat beetles that zoom around the living room like small bombers from the Second World War. When one of these came to visit one day everyone scattered in different directions, I had never seen people move so fast. Tom and Connor shut themselves in a bedroom while Frank, the brave man of the house, shot off the other way, leaving the only female member of the clan to swish out the unwanted visitor. As I hunted around for an old newspaper, Connor came flying out the bedroom carrying a floppy plastic sword from his toy box. Brandishing his weapon in the air he looked like a brave strong warrior, come to save his mother from alien monsters. He did in fact thrust the sword roughly in my direction then race back to hide in the wardrobe, slamming the door behind him, and wailing at the top of his voice. I was then obviously supposed to kill the beast with a limp piece of plastic that masqueraded as a deadly weapon. What I really did was gently persuade the animal to leave via the patio door, using a rolled up paper and a few expletives.

* * *

We took Connor to Spain recently on a ferry as we had no one to look after the dog for the summer, and couldn't bear, or afford, to put her in kennels for that long. He found it confusing, and a little hard to cope with the change in his expectations. The drive down south to the ferry went off okay, but when we arrived at the port he started yelling for the plane. He had no idea that the ship would take us to the same place, and we couldn't seem to make him understand. Not wishing to commence a twenty-five hour crossing on choppy seas with a screaming child, I said that it was a "boat plane" and luckily for us he calmed down and seemed to accept that explanation. We found our cabin, retrieved the dog from the car and took her up to the kennels. Connor seemed to find this quite amusing, and we stayed up there with her while the ferry left port, watching England disappear off into the distance. There was a small play room next to the dining hall so he played there for a while, then went back to our room to find his colouring pens and DVD's. Unfortunately the weather soon turned nasty, and visiting Toffee on the top deck was like walking into a tornado. Not being a big fan of ferries at the best of times, I clung onto the rails like my life depended on it, wondering why I'd agreed to this in the first place. By 6pm, both boys were lying on their bunks, a nice shade of green, watching the rain beating against the porthole. Rather bored by now, Frank went to the bar, while I sat with the boys, praying for them to go to sleep before one of them threw up. Only eighteen more hours to go, great. We made it to Spanish soil, and then faced a ten-hour drive to the house, arriving at exactly midnight. The holiday came with the usual trials and tribulations you faced with Connor, then it was time to repeat the process in reverse. We stopped for a night in Madrid, not wanting to endure the long drive in one go again, and luckily there was a McDonalds near the hotel so he was happy and full. It was then back on the ferry for another twenty odd hours of torture. Happily the weather was better this time and no one was ill, until Tom regurgitated his cereal all over the carpet in the food hall the next morning. The ferry had a small cinema on board and were showing the latest Shrek movie, which Tom wanted to see. We agonised over whether we could persuade Connor to join us, given his hatred of going to the pictures. Tom and I went to have a look, and found that it only contained seven rows of seats, forty-nine chairs in total, and was not much bigger than a large living room. Feeling confident, we purchased three tickets, with the promise of a refund if Connor decided not to come. Back at the cabin we asked him if he wanted to see Shrek in the "DVD room", and amazingly he said yes. I was ecstatic. It was years since we'd had hysterics in a cinema and he'd refused to step foot in one since. He came with us, and apart from being a little noisy and jumping about in his seat, he actually lasted through the whole film. We raced back to the room to tell Frank, so excited that he had made this huge step and that we'd been able to do something together, at last.

We continue to take Connor away, and he continues to hate it for the most part, but we need to get out of the house sometimes and at least see the sun even if we don't get to sit in it much.

# 19

## EVIL MONSTERS

Most kids, given the chance, would choose a day at home as opposed to going to school. How many of us didn't try that on at least once during our childhood. You would wake up maybe feeling a little fed up or under the weather, but not really ill enough to warrant a day off. Crawling downstairs, still wrapped in your quilt, you would manage a pathetic croak of a voice in the hope of gaining some sympathy. A sore stomach or feeling nauseous was always favourite, as the symptoms are easy to fake and hard to disprove. Having a raised temperature was a little trickier to pull off. If you were lucky and your Mum believed you, you got a day in jarmies in front of the TV, being waited on hand and foot. Only snag is that trying this trick once too often can backfire when you really are ill, as I found out one day. I had been sent to school, despite repeated protests that I was feeling very sick. I must have looked ill as the music teacher offered to drive me home immediately after registration. As he and my Mum were chatting at the door I made a dash for the bathroom, but it was too late. I threw my guts up all over the stair carpet that had just been cleaned.

Connor, thankfully, hasn't learnt the art of deception yet. He doesn't have the skills required to pretend he has a headache or feign a sore tummy. Instead he prefers a much more honest approach. If he doesn't fancy school one day he just screams and shouts at the top of his voice to let you know. Luckily the process of ripping his uniform back off after a long fight to get it on seems to have ceased now, but he stills likes to get his point across about not wanting to go. He yells as loud as he can "NO, NO SCHOOL, EVIL MONSTERS!" No one is spared this insult. I get it for making him go, the taxi driver and escort get it for taking him there, and his teachers get it, for well, just being his teachers. It is all taken in good spirits; no one takes this verbal abuse to heart. It is, in fact, quite amusing as all the staff are so lovely, they are the furthest thing from evil monsters you could possibly get.

On a few occasions the nurse has phoned to say that Connor has a raging temperature, they have tried and failed to get any medication in to him and would I come and pick him up. I would drop what I was doing and rush to the school; sick bucket at the ready, fully expecting an emergency visit to the doctor would be necessary. I would find him lying still on the nurses' bed, as white as the sheet he was on, and half asleep. He would be hot and clammy and only have enough energy to whisper the words "time to go home". Feeling so sorry for him I would gently scoop him up and carry him out to the car. He would sit quietly all the way home, staring forlornly out of the window. Within the hour you would never have guessed he had been ill at all. He would be drinking juice, singing loudly, and stuffing down pieces of toast. Maybe he can recover very quickly, or maybe he was just having us all on. It makes me wonder if he is much smarter than we give him credit for.

* * *

Dare to ask Connor anything about school and you get firmly put in your place. The answer is always the same, no matter what question you put to him.

Did you have fun at school today? – "NO"

Did you go swimming today (when you know he did)? – "NO, NO"

Did you eat your dinner (lunchbox comes back empty)? – "NO,NO,NO!"

He wants to forget all about the dreaded place when he comes home; even the mere mention of the word infuriates him. If you say it at the weekend there is murder. On a really bad day he will draw a 'NO ENTRY' sign and stick it to the front door the correct way round so as to be visible from the outside. When we open the door to the escort she gets showered with insults, all reasonably polite, as luckily he hasn't picked up any really bad ones yet. After being shouted at to "GET OUT OF MY HOUSE!" she just laughs, and leads him out to the car.

Monday mornings tend to be worst, especially after a holiday. Things improve throughout the week, and by Friday he happily gives me a big kiss before running off down the path. When the weekend is over, the cycle begins all over again. If I dare to lay out his uniform on a Sunday night, or even iron it in front of him on a non-school day, I get a severe telling off. It must then be hidden out of sight, to put an end to the yelling.

* * *

The staff do their very best to accommodate each child's specific needs and desires. There are only around eight to ten children in each class, with one teacher and two assistants, and just over eighty in the whole school, but the range of disabilities is huge and varying. No two children can be categorised as being alike, they all have different skills and abilities, even if they suffer from the same condition as one another. It is the teachers' job to seek out and identify these attributes, having to structure each lesson in such a way that stimulates, engages, and educates each and every pupil in the group. The lessons have to be short and to the point, as the concentration spans are extremely limited, but the patience required to teach the same subject to a class of completely different children is immense.

Being a school governor, I have had the chance to sit in on some of these sessions. Whenever outside authorities come in to evaluate the teachers, they often ask a governor to accompany them. I jump at the chance, as much as it still saddens me to see these young people dealing with such debilitating problems, it is equally as lifting to witness them learning new skills with a smile on their face.

Classes are split roughly according to age or attainment level, but each child may have a completely different disability. Getting this mix right can't always be easy, and the school are the first to admit that this sometimes comes down to trial and error. Autistic children can find it extremely hard to get along with others, and in Connors' case there have been personality clashes in the past. He had to be moved out of one group because he was being physically attacked by two of the other boys, and couldn't stand up to them, or fight back. Months later, they had to remove another child out of the class Connor was in due to them having a real dislike of each other, but on the whole things have gone smoothly. He has been with the same teacher for four years now, as he is happy and responds well to them. Any issues we have had have been dealt with swiftly and compassionately, Connors' needs being put first every time.

To teach the children social skills and how to behave appropriately, they take them out into the community on a regular basis. These trips give them the opportunity to practise every day skills such as choosing an item in a shop and paying for it themselves. Even visiting an unfamiliar place and having to talk to a stranger is a huge and daunting task for a child like Connor. These seemingly small, but very important skills are an essential part of growing up and gaining some amount of independence.

The class visited a local church one day and were astonished at Connors' reaction. He immediately put on the robes, stood in the pulpit with arms outstretched, and gave a sermon to an empty room. They had no idea what he was saying, but were totally convinced that we must take Connor to church each Sunday, as he knew exactly what to do. I had to confess that we had never actually taken him, for fear of him causing complete havoc during a service as he is incapable of sitting still or keeping quiet, but we were amused by his actions.

A few years ago they were often writing in his home/school book, delighting in the fact that he was so well behaved when he went out on a trip. I wrote back, begging for some guidance, as he was always escaping from me, they must have discovered some special way of controlling him that I hadn't thought of. I was really excited, imagining some ingenious method that I could adopt to make trips out less stressful. It transpired that they did have their own approach, but it wasn't at all what I was expecting. The teacher replied to my inquiry, stating that when she took him out he was strapped into a buggy for the majority of the time. I was absolutely livid. I phoned the school to say that I didn't wish to cause trouble, but I couldn't see how restraining a very active little boy would teach him anything about how to conduct himself in public. I understood it was difficult, I had chased him at full speed around so many places I had lost count, but this couldn't be the answer. I offered to either keep him home on days when the class were going out, or better still I would go with them. I would be wholly responsible for his actions, but I strongly felt that locking him in a chair was not helping anyone. The deputy head agreed with me, and assured us that this would never happen again. I know that teacher was only concerned for his safety, but had she sought to consult me first, we could have come up with an acceptable alternative for us all.

* * *

The first time I got to see the whole school together was for sports day. Connor had joined the reception class in early June, so had only been there a matter of weeks. As the children all need constant supervision, it was the visitors' responsibility to watch them during the afternoon. Luckily my parents were able to come with me as I was on crutches after a foot operation, and wasn't in any fit state to chase him around. I hobbled across the playground and found three spare chairs, not that we needed them all for long. The minute Connor appeared he rushed over for a cuddle, and a delve through my bag to see if I'd brought him anything. He sat contentedly on my knee for the few minutes it took him to gulp down some juice, then he was off. Excited at being allowed to run free, he explored the grounds with my poor Mum and Dad having to take it in turns to follow. I felt guilty just sitting there, but with broken bones in both feet I couldn't move very fast. He came to sit down on a few occasions, but this only lasted seconds and he was off again for another circuit of the field. As I sat and watched the others taking part in their races I couldn't help but feel overwhelmed with emotion. To see little children bravely racing up and down in wheelchairs, or holding on to frames to keep them steady, just sliced my heart in two. It just didn't seem fair that they were having to cope with such huge problems at such a young age. I was grateful that it was a hot afternoon so I had the chance to hide behind my sunglasses. When it was Connors' turn to run he had to be led firmly by the hand to the starting line. One of the teaching assistants ran with him, encouraging him to take part, but he was having none of it. He fought and yelled until he broke free from her grip, and was off up the hill again in seconds. He had no idea what he was supposed to be doing, and no interest in conforming whatsoever. We gave up and decided to leave him be. They tried to keep to the plan as much as possible, but it was slightly chaotic, with some running the wrong way or in the wrong races, but they were all having fun regardless so it didn't matter one bit. At the end they each received a medal whether they had won anything or not. In Connors' case he got his for merely showing up.

* * *

The annual Christmas play is equally as difficult to watch. All the children get involved in some way or another, and even those in chairs dress up and are wheeled around to the music. A huge amount of effort goes into planning these productions and every member of staff wears a costume and joins in enthusiastically. Connor has never been too impressed with all the fuss though. He spent the first few years refusing to even venture out of the classroom, and was the only member of the school who wouldn't take part. Then for the next two years he made a brief appearance, but refused to put on his costume. Last Christmas was the only time he has actually participated fully; he dressed up and carried out the actions he was supposed to do. Once he'd spotted Tom and me though that was it. He rushed over to sit with us and stayed there for the rest of the performance. Tom has asked to come with me, and I had gained permission for him to be off for the afternoon. I was pleased he wanted to, and he used to find visiting Connors' school very distressing. He often inquired as to what was wrong with each child and I would explain as best I could, but it was a lot for a young boy to take in. he had followed some of the children's' progress from when they started in reception to where they are now, and comments on the changes he sees in them. He noted that one little boy was no longer attached to an oxygen cylinder, and another could now walk better. Seeing such a different side of life has been a good lesson for Tom, and makes him grateful that he is healthy himself. Having Connor as a brother has been extremely hard at times, but it has made Tom a much more caring and compassionate individual. If more young mainstream educated children got to visit special needs schools it might just turn them into more understanding adults in the future.

* * *

Right now Connor is cooperating well, and working hard at his studies. Progress is painfully slow, but at least he is moving in the right direction. His reading, writing, and drawing skills have reached a level I once feared he could never achieve, and he is now learning to put a full stop at the end of a sentence. It took him four years to learn how to sit through an assembly, and four years to realise the objectives of sports day. He continues to detest school discos, and only tolerates the summer fair as they have a toy stall he can rummage through. It is only very recently that he has agreed to sit with the group on a Monday morning and discuss what they all did over the weekend. He remains extremely stubborn and determined, each lesson being a battle of wills he can't be allowed to win. Lately they have been teaching simple mathematics to the class. When I asked him at home what one plus one was, he answered "Lego". Obviously we still have some way to go.

As much as it still hurts to acknowledge that my own son needs to attend such a complex special needs establishment, it is also comforting to know that he is safe there. He is very well looked after, learning steadily, and is constantly monitored and can't possibly escape. We could have fought for him to go to a mainstream school with one-to-one assistance, but I know he would never have coped in such an environment. Whenever I attend Toms' assemblies, sports days, or end of year school productions, I can't help but leave with a lump in my throat. I so wish Connor could be there, joining in with the rest of the children, but I know he is better off where he is. He is protected from those who may try to exploit his naivety and vulnerability. In Connors' world there is no prejudice, distinction, or segregation. The children there simply accept each other for who and what they are.

# 20

## THE TOOTH FAIRY

A massive problem we still haven't managed to make much progress with is Connors' dental hygiene. He will brush his own teeth with just water, but dare to go anywhere near him with tooth paste and all hell breaks loose. The mere sight of the stuff sends him running at full speed out of the bathroom. I have tried them all, from mild mint paste and cherry flavoured gels to animal shaped brushes dipped in mouthwash. I have bought every make, every colour, every flavour and every texture I can find, but nothing gets past Connors' excellent detection system. Just like with food, everything has to be touched, smelt and vetted before it is deemed edible. Nothing that isn't bland, boring or tasteless gets through his defences.

In a desperate attempt to save his teeth I used to sneak up on him from behind and ram in the toothbrush before he realised what was going on. We would then end up in a heap on the floor, with me on top just managing to cling on to the handle while he flung his head wildly from side to side. If he didn't manage to pull out the brush he would clamp his teeth tightly around it so I couldn't move it around. It was then a standoff, a battle of wills and strength, and eventually I would concede defeat and withdraw. He would cry, and spit, and yell abuse at me and I was mortified about doing that to him, but I really was faced with no alternative. If he was to have any teeth left by the time he reached adulthood, then we had to find a way of getting some fluoride into his mouth. Eventually, I gave up this method as it was upsetting him too much and did nothing to help him stay calm on a school day. Forcing his uniform on was bad enough, trying to clean his teeth as well was a step too far.

Even when he accepted the idea of brushing with water only, we knew it was not going to be enough. Better than nothing, certainly, but still no replacement for the protection provided by the ingredients contained in toothpaste. It was essential a better solution be found. For various reasons we decided to change dentists, and the first time we took him he happily went into the consulting room. He allowed a very quick glance in his mouth then refused to cooperate any further. Positive that he was suffering from toothache, as he had been recently holding his face in his hands, we asked to be referred to a local clinic that was better prepared for treating 'difficult' patients.

As usual, Frank was away on business, so I had to face this visit alone. With my wonderful sense of direction I drove past the place three times before deciding which building it was. Of course, as is the case for many hospitals and clinics in this country, the few parking spaces that were available were all occupied so we ended up half a mile down the road. The anxiety levels were already high as I anticipated yet another stressful trip out, and now, to add insult to injury, I was late and didn't want to miss our slot. Connor, already sensing he was going somewhere unpleasant, wasn't at all pleased about being dragged along the road at full speed. At last we reached the door and went in. I queued at the reception desk to give in his name and he wandered off in search of anything that may be remotely interesting. Once he was ticked off on the list I was advised to take a seat, not that there were any of those left either. The place was heaving with parents and fed up children, and as I weaved my way through the crowd in a futile attempt to find somewhere to sit I realised that yet again we were in for a long wait. Our appointment time actually meant nothing at all, everyone was told to arrive at the start of the session and then it was a lottery as to when your name would be called. You just had to patiently wait your turn like everyone else who was there that day. Don't get me wrong, this is fine if you have a child who can manage to wait, who can calmly sit and listen to a story or play quietly with a favourite toy, but being patient, calm, or quiet is an abstract concept to Connor. Not expecting to be there for any length of time, I stupidly hadn't taken much for him to do, not that any amount of toys would have kept him occupied for long anyway. In places such as this, Connors' favourite pastime is to explore. In his mind, closed doors are there to be opened, cupboards are there to be emptied, and corridors make wonderful places to run. Having spent a few minutes eyeing up the other kids' toys, he came to his first door. Before I could grab him he was through it and gone, hurtling off down the hall to see what he could find. We visited people in their offices, surprised at being suddenly disturbed by a silent child and his apologetic mother. He barged into a few surgeries where patients were being seen, before I arm wrestled him to the floor and marched him back to the main waiting area. We had only been there about fifteen minutes but it felt like much longer. Spotting a vacant chair I grabbed it and forced Connor onto my knee. I gave him the one drink I had brought from home and we looked through some books, which seemed to placate him for a short while. Quickly bored though, he jumped off and decided to do another circuit of the room. Not wanting to lose my precious seat, I stayed put as I could survey his whereabouts from where I was. He appeared quite happy and didn't seem to be causing any trouble, so I left him to wander. If I tried to get him back on my lap I knew it would only end in a loud tantrum and we had already attracted enough attention as it was. Lowering my guard for a second, I dared to look down at my magazine. Glancing up moments later, I was just in time to see Connor hovering over the stand-alone black board that was located near the entrance. Written on it were all the weeks sessions, with days of the week, times, and dentists names, all neatly laid out and colour coded. Sadly, it was too much for him to resist, and with one big sweep of his bare arm he wiped the whole board clean. It had probably taken someone a good while to write, but it only took Connor a second to remove the lot. Everyone stopped and stared at him in utter disbelief and silence. The girls on reception hadn't noticed and were going about their business as normal. I stared too, frozen to my chair in shock, not quite sure what to do. It would have been lovely to pretend he wasn't with me, but I didn't have that luxury. Hanging my head in shame, not wishing to catch anyone's eye, I darted over to where he was standing. He appeared quite satisfied, content with the fact that he had cleared the board of all the messy chalk marks and it was now blank and ready to be used again. I pulled him over to the desk to make a grovelling apology, and crawled back to my seat with an angry, writhing, child clamped tightly by both hands. The staff were really not amused that their work had been ruined and I cringed with the embarrassment of it all. As I held him tightly on my knee, the yelling getting louder and louder as he fought to escape, I could feel the tears welling inside. I was angry and frustrated at being put through yet another horrendous clinic visit with no one there willing to help. I had warned them when our own dentist had made this appointment. Had explained in explicit detail about past visits to health centres and how he reacted when expected to behave in a room full of strangers. I told them he would want to run away and escape at the first opportunity; had pleaded with them not to send me somewhere where we would have to wait for any length of time. I was assured that his needs would be taken in to account and that my concerns had been duly noted. Obviously, nothing I said had been taken seriously, and they probably thought I was over reacting or being too fussy.

We had been there for well over an hour when finally his name was called. Everyone must have breathed a sigh of relief when we disappeared off down the corridor. When we entered a room the screaming subsided as he eyed up all the shiny objects laid out on the counters. It was a large area with three consulting chairs to choose from so he tried them all, content for a moment to ride up and down, sitting up and lying back using the electronic controls manned by one of the nurses. He twirled round and round on all the office style seats and happily played with the sterilised instruments that had been neatly set out on metal trays. The nurse chased after him, assuring me that they were used to this kind of behaviour, while I gave the dentist a brief history of his health. After about ten minutes of chasing he stayed still long enough to allow them a fleeting look with the mirror. The dentist thought that he had at least one tooth that needed to be extracted, possibly two, but it was difficult to tell with all the jumping about. She concluded that his needs would be better met at the paediatric dental department located in our local hospital and once sedated, they could have a good look around and do all the necessary work in one go. I nodded in agreement, past caring by now, just wanting to get out and go home and leave the trauma of that visit behind, not to mention all the contaminated instruments that would require autoclaving all over again.

* * *

I called on my parents for help the next time, not wishing to face another traumatic episode alone. As there was nowhere to park, and we had no idea how long we'd be, my Dad drove us to the hospital and my Mum came in with me. Yet again I'd been advised that the staff were well used to dealing with children with autism and his needs would be catered for, and yet again they were wrong. This time at least there were fewer people waiting to be seen, and there was a small play area providing limited amusement, but it was blatantly apparent that we all had the same appointment slot and you just had to wait your turn in the queue. He was calmer and better behaved this time, and after visiting a few offices and legging up and down the nearest corridor, he tolerated sitting in the waiting room while my Mum and I amused him as best we could. The staff were very caring though, periodically checking that we were okay and assuring us that the wait wouldn't be too long. After about forty-five minutes it was our turn. I was asked to go in with

Connor and my Mum was told to wait outside. I felt calm and confident that all would go well. I assumed, wrongly as it turned out, that he would be given a small injection to send him drifting off to sleep with the least amount of stress. Unfortunately though, that wasn't the plan. I was ordered to sit in the chair with Connor on my knee and hold down his arms so he couldn't break free or hit out at anyone. They then produced a mask and held it over his face to gas him to sleep. It seemed to take an eternity, only about fifteen to twenty seconds actually, but with him screaming and throwing his body around and me having to take his weight, and the weight of two other people who were lying on top in an attempt to stop him taking off the mask, it felt like much longer. Once asleep everyone jumped off and I was extracted from underneath and escorted out the door. I stood on the other side, trying to catch my breath and take in the events of the last half a minute. I was horrified that he had had to endure that terror of not understanding what was happening to him or why. I remembered being gassed to sleep in the dentists' chair as a child, and it wasn't pleasant, but at least I had known what was coming, and was mentally prepared for it. We couldn't explain to Connor that it was for his own good, and that it would take away the pain from his bad tooth. He had no idea why he was there or what they intended to do to him. He may have thought they were trying to hurt him, and he was literally fighting for his life. I headed straight for the ladies room, not trusting myself to go back to my Mum for fear of breaking down. I took some deep breaths trying to calm myself, but even before I had finished washing my hands there was a bang on the door. It was over, and Connor was already starting to come round from the anaesthetic. I was ushered into the recovery room and he was wheeled out half asleep. My Mum came in from the waiting area and we were given a box of tissues and left alone. He was obviously very upset and traumatised and was crying bitterly, even before he was fully conscious. With tears streaming down his face, and thick red blood pouring out of his mouth, he clung tightly to me. He spluttered and spat all down my top as I tried in vain to catch as much as I could with the tissues, and he took short sharp breaths as he struggled to regain composure. It took a good fifteen to twenty minutes for him to calm down enough to allow us to clean his face. By now the next patient was ready for recovery and we had to leave. We were shown out through another door and found ourselves in the corridor outside. You obviously weren't allowed back through the dental department for fear of upsetting the other children still waiting. I phoned my Dad and we drove home in virtual silence, all of us shocked and upset by what Connor had just endured. I made a promise to him that I would never put him through anything like that again, but the saga of his teething troubles was still far from over.

A year or so later, after another disastrous visit to our own dentist, it was decided that he needed another extraction. Refusing to go back to the same clinic I asked to be referred to the nearest children's hospital, in the hope that they would be more used to dealing with cases such as Connors'.

First we had to go for a consultation where they assured us that he would be put to sleep by injection as opposed to gas. A few weeks later Connor and I stayed the night at my parents, as we had an early appointment and their house was only a short drive away. As he couldn't eat before having a general anaesthetic we woke him up at the last possible moment and bundled him into the car before he had the chance to protest. On arriving at the hospital we located the correct department and registered his name. Again it was pretty busy, and again everyone was set to arrive at the same time and wait their turn. At least though, there were plenty of toys and games to distract him, and all the other children were making as much noise as Connor. He ran around and played happily for about ten to fifteen minutes then a member of staff came over to prepare him for the surgery. He tolerated having the anaesthetic cream on the back of his hands quite well, but was less than amused by the identity wrist band. I did explain that this could cause a problem, but was told that every child was required to have one, and there would be no exceptions made. They couldn't risk getting anyone mixed up, which I fully understood, but they hadn't been on the receiving end of one of Connors' tantrums, yet. We tried our best to distract him, but having this foreign object wrapped around his arm was too much for him to bear. He would forget about it for a few minutes then start yelling and frantically pulling at the band in an attempt to rip it off. As they are specifically designed not to tear, the offending item stood its ground, and Connor was getting angrier by the second. Realising that neither my mum nor I was willing to help him, he kept running over to the nurses and grabbing their arms in a desperate attempt to get their attention, but he was totally ignored by all the staff. Half an hour passed with him yelling and racing around the waiting room, and I was beginning to feel rather distressed myself. Eventually one nurse seemed to take pity on us and came over brandishing a large pair of scissors. With one snip the problem was solved. Once free of his band he ran off contentedly to play as if nothing had happened. When it was his turn for a pre-med, he was laid down in a bed and given the medicine via a syringe. I had warned them that this was not going to be an easy task, and a fair bit got spat out, but enough was swallowed to calm him down. We then were taken to a small soft-play room so we could be alone and Connor could relax. He rolled about the floor and was unsteady on his feet, so we knew that the medication was beginning to work. After another half hour he was put on a trolley to go up in the lift to the theatres on the top floor. He thought this was great fun and cuddled down in the sheets, pulling the blanket up around his neck. Once they had fully sedated him I was sent back downstairs to wait on the ward. They told us he would be up there for probably an hour, so we could have a cup of tea and breathe a sigh of relief.

When I was summoned back up he was awake and crying. As he was bleeding quite heavily, he had to stay in recovery for a while longer, but eventually the blood flow subsided and we were allowed back down to join my mum. A few hours later he was given the all clear, and we phoned my dad, relieved to escape and put the trauma of the visit behind us. On our way out I decided to grab a few of the cardboard sick bowls, not expecting to need them, but just in case.

After giving him a few hours to recover, I left my parents house for the forty-minute drive home. Connor sat next to me in the front seat, rather tired, pale and quiet, but that was understandable given the day he'd had. He snuggled down in his blanket and dropped off to sleep for a little while. As I neared the house, I was forced to stop at a junction as the traffic lights turned red. Connor woke up, and as I looked across at him I knew he was about to vomit. Not being able to trust him to hold the bowl himself, I quickly grabbed one off the floor and held it under his chin. Just in time as it happened. As he hadn't eaten much that day it was mostly liquid, but lots of it. He filled the container to the top, and any slight movement would have sent it slopping over the edge onto the floor of my car. Not wishing to smell that for the next six months, I was in a dilemma. I needed to get out of the door without spilling a drop, but was still strapped in, and was in a long queue of traffic. As the lights had changed people were beeping me from behind, trying to get past. Didn't they know I was balancing a bowl of puke in one hand, whilst attempting to undo my seat belt with the other? Still having no idea how I

323

managed it; I extracted myself from my chair and deposited the contents of Connor's stomach safely on a grass verge, without losing so much as a drip.

* * *

Despite our best efforts we have made little progress with the teeth hygiene since that day, and I fear that before long we will have to make the dreaded journey to the hospital again. He has been assigned a special needs dentist now, and they are very patient with him, but he still won't let them do more than probe around with a mirror and a dry brush. I wish that a toothpaste manufacturer could develop a product with no smell or taste, and then we might have a fighting chance of overcoming this very big problem.

# 21

## TODAY IS A GIFT

*"Yesterday is History*

*Tomorrow is Mystery*

*Today is a Gift"*

(ELEANOR ROOSEVELT)

I love this saying, but I have to come clean and confess that I first heard it from wise old master Oogway in the summer of 2008. For those who are perhaps somewhat unfamiliar with the ins and outs of children's films, he is the old master in 'Kung Fu Panda'. He is trying to teach the rather overweight, clueless Panda some lessons in life. I am ashamed to say that I didn't know who had actually written this quote, until I found it on a fridge magnet months later in a bookstore in America. It now has pride of place on my new fridge freezer in the kitchen and I make a point of stopping to read it often. To ponder over its powerful message condensed down into those few short, but very meaningful, lines. You see for me, it sums up perfectly my struggle with Connor and his autism over the years.

For a long time I was trapped in the past, unable to move on or let go. My whole life centred around Connor, and what trying to cope with him did to me both physically and mentally. I was totally exhausted, on edge, irritable and probably not so nice to be around a lot of the time. If he wound me up or drove me to tears, which was most days, I would rant and rave about it down the phone to Frank. Luckily he worked away from home for the most part, so didn't have to live with my constant hysterical outbursts. I could recall every episode, every tantrum, every horrendous trip out, and every stare from strangers who were horrified at the dreadful behaviour of this young child and his useless mother. I would cry tears of frustration and despair for many, many hours. Entirely convinced that he was so badly behaved and horrible to me on purpose. That he somehow cleverly planned his moves to create the biggest impact possible. The more bizarre and daring his behaviour; the bigger the reaction from me. I really believed for a long time that he hated me, and I was mortified.

People often ask me how I cope with him and his disability. I feel that at the age he is now, he is at the most easiest stage of his life so far, in terms of his behaviour management. The past was pretty tough I must admit, but I am slowly learning to put it to the back of my mind. When others say that they think I cope very well, I take it as a good sign. But most of them didn't know us years ago when he was at his worst. I can laugh now about some of the crazy things he has done, but at the time I was a complete mess. Yesterday is indeed history, and you can't alter the past. I need to leave all those feelings, emotions and anxieties far, far behind and look ahead. Right now I live for the present, trying not to dwell on the past, but also attempting not to worry about the future. It will be the same anyway, regardless of how much I fret about it, regardless of how many sleepless nights I suffer, regardless of the number of tears I shed. Yes, he will undoubtedly be a challenging teenager when all the hormones kick in, and he grows too big and strong for me to physically restrain, but we will face that when it happens, just as we have faced everything else up to now.

I love to spend time with Connor and enjoy his company; something I thought might never be possible. He also takes great pleasure in being close

327

to us, both physically and emotionally. He adores hugs and cuddles from those he loves, and will even sit on the knee of someone he barely knows if he fancies it. During my years of running the fundraising committee of Toms' school, I had many female visitors round to the house for meetings. Connor would wander in and sit on a nice looking knee to see what it felt like. My unsuspecting guest would then receive a soft stroke on the arm or leg before he jumped off and disappeared once more. Luckily no one seemed to mind this physical invasion by inquisitive, cold little hands. I was just relieved that he didn't do to them what he still insists on doing to me. That is sneaking a hand up inside your top to feel what is in there. I am trying to teach him that this behaviour is unacceptable now he is older, but I fear the message will take a long time to sink in.

The problem is he adores the feel of bare skin. Around 6am each morning I am woken by tiny arms engulfing my middle. He wraps everything he can tightly around me. A bony knee gets rammed hard in to my full bladder and wandering fingers dig down deep in to my bellybutton. After fruitless attempts to throw him off I give in graciously. Not wanting to rise for at least another hour, I let him have his fix. He also loves stomach-to-stomach contact. He pulls up my top and his own, then belly flops on to me to rub them together. This I am attempting to wean him off as well.

I can look back now with more clarity, I think for a while I got lost somewhere along the way. Forgetting that we were actually a whole family fighting to come to terms with a terrible shock. It wasn't just me, everyone else around me was involved too, but on a day-to-day basis I felt very much alone and very, very afraid. Afraid of each day and what it might bring. Afraid of the future and what it could hold, and sometimes afraid of myself, of my own reactions and insecurities. Afraid that one day I would just snap and totally lose control. Not be able to go on and lash out at the very people that surrounded me and were trying to help.

Learning your child has the lifelong disability of autism has been described to me as akin to coping with the grief of losing a loved one. The child you thought you had, who appeared perfectly normal when born, has now gone, never to return. But you are unable to grieve and then move on with your life as you are faced with a living, breathing, very unpredictable and energetic little person. These children need twenty-four hour care, and have many complex needs and problems. They are unable to cope with day-to-day life like normal children, and can find the world a very scary and confusing place to live. They have bizarre behaviour patterns and terrible communication barriers, and find learning even the simplest of things almost impossible.

When a parent at Toms' school heard about Connor she said to me that every child is a precious miracle. I was more than a little annoyed with the comment at first. I thought - that's easy for you to say, when you have two children without any problems. Two children, who lead a normal life, go to mainstream school, can make friends, talk, play, and fit in. She didn't even know me very well at all. Had no idea what I had to put up with, had no clue what my life was like, and no notion of how much stress I was under. But I think now she probably just didn't know what else to say, and she was actually right.

It is indeed a privilege to be able to have a child. Sadly, due to varying reasons, many couples simply can't, and many babies are lost at birth or by miscarriage. So to be blessed with this gift is something to celebrate. I must enjoy Connor the way he is now, and forget all the terrible times I have had with him. After all, life is so fragile and can be taken away in the blink of an eye. Ten years ago I was diagnosed with a serious heart condition, and given less than a year to live. Luckily I was able to undergo an operation which cured the problem, and saved my life. I was given a second chance, should be grateful, and make the most of it.

I was once asked if we knew that Connor had autism before he was born, was there any way of testing for it? Obviously my answer was no, we had no clue, and there were no tests. But what if there had been? What would we have done with that knowledge? In a way I'm glad there wasn't, I would have spent my whole life wondering if we had made the right decision, whichever path we had chosen to take. Regardless of his faults, regardless of how exhausting life is with him, he loves us dearly and we feel the same back.

As the saying goes – don't dwell on the past, enjoy today, and the future is still unwritten.

# 22

## TIME WAITS FOR NO MAN

I think we'd all like to turn back the clock, slow down the passage of time, and discover the secret of eternal youth. We'd like our bodies and minds to remain forever young and vibrant, but sadly we all have to grow up and grow old in the end. There is only so much one can achieve through the wonders of cosmetic surgery, delaying yes, but not stopping the inevitable. But can we successfully keep our minds young, even if our bodies race on ahead? Surely, after all, we are only as old as we feel?

I have discovered that having children is a terrific way of being able to re-live your own childhood without appearing stupid or immature. My boys have so much more to play with than we did at their age. There just wasn't all the hand held electronic devices, sophisticated computer games, plug and play TV consoles, or interactive DVDs. They hadn't been invented then. When my brother got his first computer I was fascinated, it was a very basic 'Sinclair' model, if I remember correctly. We played games of tennis, but not with people, crowds or even a net in sight. Your 'player' was a short black line you could move up and down one side of the screen, and the 'ball' was a tiny black square that was hit between the two lines. If you gave that to a modern day child they would throw it at you, but back then we thought it was genius.

The invention of the Nintendo Wii has taken things to a new level completely. There is virtually nothing you can't do on that, and all the family can play games together. Even Connor has become really interested in this, and will play happily alongside Tom and his friends. He is not daft though, as he often insists on me joining in when they play 'Mario Kart' racing. Not because he loves me so much that he wants me with him, it is only for the fact that I am so bad I will come last, which means that he can't lose the races himself.

* * *

A question often asked of young children is "What do you want to be when you grow up?" Many have an idea of who they'd like to aspire to, even if it ends up as a totally unrealistic or unachievable goal in the end.

Little boys hope of becoming airline pilots, professional footballers or famous rock stars. Girls may dream of being a ballerina, fashion model or a beautiful princess. As they grow up though their priorities and expectations will alter as reality kicks in. Teenage boys will drool over the scantily clad models they see in magazines, and the mere sight of a burly fireman in uniform is enough to send a young woman's heart racing. Some of us though, have enough determination and belief to achieve the goals we invented during our childhood. I never had any idea what I wanted to be, what young girl dreams of becoming an accountant, for heaven's sake?

* * *

These days we tend to keep a much closer eye on our children than generations before us. We lock them in behind closed doors, not allowing them to play out in the street, walk themselves to school, or even cross the road unaccompanied. We wrap them up in cotton wool, convinced that something dreadful will happen if we so much as divert our eyes for a second. Not all of our insecurities are fictional though; society has changed over the years, and not always in a good way. But eventually they reach an age where we really need to take a step back and give them some independence. You set boundaries and stipulate rules, but they need to learn to stand on their own two feet and make some decisions for themselves.

I fear though, that we will never be able to afford Connor the amount of freedom you could give a so-called 'normal' child. His body is maturing and growing older at the right speed, but his mind is being left far behind. He shows great signs of having plenty of intelligence, and a huge capacity to learn, but his social and communication skills are still that of a very young child. His autism affects all aspects of his development, and is a barrier that is impossible to break down. He remains as naive and vulnerable as a two year old, and therefore requires that level of supervision. But we can't live our lives being negative all the time; it really isn't healthy for any of us. He has made great progress in many areas of his life, and we have to cling to the belief that this will continue. We have to focus on the positive, expand his knowledge, and exploit his strengths.

Connor has achieved lots of the things we once thought may be beyond his grasp. He can read well, pronouncing many a difficult word correctly, but only when he can be bothered to do so. He will only read stories that he chooses himself, and quickly gets angry if I try to interest him in something else, but a favourite book can get read over and over again with him inventing different voices for each character. He can hold a pen properly and his writing is neat and legible; he is able to spell many words correctly, and will attempt those he finds challenging. The biggest stumbling block we have is getting him to stay still and sit down for long enough to do anything. Connor would much rather be watching TV or bouncing on his trampoline than reading and writing, but these are essential skills which need to be constantly developed and improved upon. One of his favourite activities right now is drawing and colouring. He is very articulate, and each picture has to be accurately drawn and coloured in the exact shades. He takes great care and pride in his work, copying cartoon characters from magazines, a paused DVD, or even just from memory. He currently has a huge stack of papers full of hundreds of pictures, and these periodically get laid out all over his bedroom floor making it impossible for us to get in. I often find him still awake at midnight, studiously drawing in his room. He should be fast asleep by this time, but at least he is doing something constructive and educational.

He still needs a lot of help with personal hygiene, requiring constant reminders to wipe properly and wash his hands after using the toilet, and I still have to wash him in the bath. I am sure that he is more than capable of looking after himself better, but he just doesn't see the need for it and really can't be bothered. He has taught himself how to operate his

'Nintendo DS', and will concentrate intently whilst engrossed in a particular game. If he is struggling on a task he will thrust the console at me, expecting me to be able to proceed to the next level. I, on the other hand, am rather useless at this, and after a few random button clicks he whips it back and works it out for himself. He still loves to dress up, and will attempt to squeeze into costumes that are much too small for him now. Normally by this age, most children have grown out of the 'pretend' stage of their lives, but Connor still exists in a world of fantasy. He still believes that fictional characters are real, and that no harm can come to him regardless of what he does. Up until very recently he has never been able to enjoy the run up to Christmas, or look forward to his next birthday. We never dared say the word 'birthday' until the actual day itself, as the mere mention of this in advance would instigate a huge tantrum. If he heard the word, he would expect presents to magically appear that very second, and God help anyone in his way if they didn't. He struggles to understand the concept of 'time', and has absolutely no idea how long a week or a month really is. He does however, now seem to know one day from the next, so we can at least ward off an impending screaming fit by showing him when something will happen. If he wants to go to his favourite play area or buy a new toy, then I write down the names of the days and we cross them off until the desired one is reached. As he knows what 'today' and 'tomorrow' mean, this method is an effective way of keeping him calm as he sees that he will get what he wants, eventually. The desired event can't be too far away though; a week or two at the most is as long as he can wait.

We still can't pass a McDonalds restaurant without stopping for his beloved chips. I learnt the hard way one day when we went to visit a friend who lives 100 miles away in Yorkshire. My brother had stayed the night, so I dropped him off at my parents' house as it was on the way. Unfortunately, this meant passing a McDonalds, but it was early in the morning and they don't serve fries until after 10.30am. Connor, of course, didn't understand that and decided to yell for the next hour until he got tired and gave up. I drove on happily, vowing to pull in at the next motorway service station that served chips. As the next services loomed I looked out for the notice saying what they provided there, but it didn't state that there were any fast food facilities. Just as I passed the junction there was a huge 'Burger King' poster plastered on the fence, but by now it was far too late for me to pull over, and I had to keep going. On seeing this Connor erupted and started screaming at me, not being able to understand that I couldn't go back now we had missed it. Promising to stop at the next services didn't help one bit, and so Tom and I just had to sit there and endure the noise. We tried turning up the volume on the radio, but couldn't drown out the high-pitched screams coming from the back seat. A few minutes later we passed a sign for the next Burger King; we only had to put up with the yelling for another 25 miles. At last with a big bag of fries safely in his clutches, the shouting subsided. He chomped away to his heart's content, while Tom and I attempted to reinstate our hearing loss after all the commotion. When the last chip was gulped down and his stomach was full, Connor stood up and announced that it was time to go home now. My response to that was that we hadn't driven a hundred miles just to buy chips, and we weren't turning around yet.

Connors speech is still extremely limited, which is frustrating for us, as we know that talking more would open up so many opportunities for him. He would stand a much better chance of making friends if he talked to other children, and it would reduce his anxiety levels if he could communicate his needs and feelings verbally. It seems a shame, because we know that he is more than capable of talking, he just doesn't see the importance of this, and refuses to make the effort. Every so often he will surprise us by saying a whole sentence; but this only happens when he is really desperate to get his point across. The rest of the time we are lucky to get a few words, and at times he reverts back to copying what we've said rather than answering a question put to him. But I am grateful for whatever speech we get; it is a huge improvement on the pointing and yelling of years ago, when it was so hard to figure out what it was he was trying to tell us. The longer it took us to guess, the more angry and frustrated he would become. If I dare to sit down for five minutes he'll say "Mum, get back to work"!, and I'm expected to jump up that very second and get whatever it is that he wants, and I had to laugh one day when he patted the dogs behind and said "the secrets in the butt"! As a big fan of animated films, he often recalls dialogue, altering it to suit a certain situation. With Frank coming and going a lot due to work commitments, Connor is very clingy to me, and worries sometimes that I won't be there when he gets home from school. He turned to me one day as he was leaving and said "no Mummy's escape from Tweedy's Farm". This is part of a line from the movie 'Chicken Run', and was his way of telling me that I must be there when he returns that afternoon; at least it's nice to know I'm wanted. Even when I get a mouthful of abuse for sending him to school, I really don't mind, for this is a voice I once feared we would never hear.

* * *

I often look at the boys now and wonder where all the time went. It won't be long before Tom is off to secondary school, and my days of running to meet him at the school gate will be over for good. They are both growing so fast, and will more than likely be taller than me before much longer, but while Tom will be mature enough to go off and do his own thing, Connor will still need protecting. He lives in a world of make believe, full of cartoon characters and Disney films, and although he is growing older by the minute, he isn't necessarily growing up. He still expects me to be able to lift him up and carry him around like a small child; he still likes the kiddies' rides outside the supermarket, and he still loves to watch the 'Teletubbies' on TV, but every step forward, however small and seemingly insignificant, is a huge leap for Connor. After all the trials and tribulations I've faced over the years, each sign of improvement gives me hope for the future.

He is years behind children of a similar age, and is developing at a much slower pace. It took him five years to speak, seven years to get out of nappies, and eight long years to tell me he loved me, but we got there in the end.

# PART 3

## THE FUTURE...

Nobody knows what their future will be. Not one of us can accurately predict what life will throw at us. We just have to hope for the best and move on, from each chapter of our lives to the next. But most of us have hopes, that given the chance, we would like to fulfil. Many have dreams they would love to come true. We would all love to see our children grow up to be happy, healthy and strong. We dare to assume that they will do well enough at school to be able to get a decent job, and make a decent living. We want to live long enough to maybe see them get married and have their own children one day. We want to be able to take our grandchildren to the beach to build sandcastles, jump the waves, and catch tiny fish in warm shallow rock pools. Then hand them back at the end of a long day when they are tired, cranky and decidedly grubby. It is then the parent's job to remove the sand from between tiny toes, scrub dried ice cream from dirty mouths and wrestle on a fresh pair of pyjamas before they collapse into a coma and have to be carried up to bed. As a grandparent you have now earned the right to bypass this bit. You can go home to peace, tranquillity, and an uninterrupted nights' sleep.

Of course everyone's lives are different in some ways, but many will probably follow a reasonably similar predictable pattern of expectations. The future of a child with autism though can be very uncertain. The only one thing I feel sure of right now, is that life with Connor is always going to be a challenge. He will grow up and mature as we all do, and his needs and priorities will undoubtedly alter. But the game will always stay the same, with the rules constantly changing. You could visit the same places, say or do the same things, subject him to the same experiences over and over again, and his reaction would be entirely different each time. You never know where his mood will take him or how he will act. There is one thing for sure; our life will never be dull and uneventful. We will face each new challenge head on with determination and courage, and will work hard to improve Connor's overall abilities and behaviours. It will be a very long and treacherous journey full of potholes, obstacles and frustrations. You may move forward three paces one day, only to fall back two the next. But you pick yourself up, dust yourself off, mop up the tears and carry on, for really what other option is there?

Right now we have a little boy who is happy and contented one minute, then angry and distressed the next. His moods can alter dramatically from one second to the next and are completely unpredictable. He still has the mental capacity of a much younger child but the strength, fitness and body of a ten year old. He is unable to comprehend how dangerous things can be and thinks nothing of climbing high objects or using sharp scissors and knives. He rushes to the front door when the bell rings and opens it for anyone, regardless if he knows them or not. He has mastered the house alarm and can unlock almost any door. He even broke through the fence one day and was found wandering around upstairs in next doors house. Luckily they know him, and understand him well. Never make the mistake of assuming that a child with a learning difficulty is not clever, or capable of doing so many things.

When he was much younger I used to think that he really hated me. That he took a great delight in making my life a living hell, and enjoyed winding me up. I think back then we all only existed in his world for one purpose, to satisfy his needs and desires and not those of our own. I am surprised that

I have any vocal cords left the amount of yelling I did in the past. When we first found out that Connor had autism our whole world fell apart. I have learnt to be more optimistic now, but still have to be realistic. He may not achieve what most children do, may never be able to get a job, fall in love, drive a car, or live independently. But we mustn't forget how far we have come already. Years ago we thought we had a child who might never talk, write, spell, sing, look us in the eye, or say 'I love you'.

Writing this book has helped me let go of the past, exorcise the demons that have haunted me for so long. I feel stronger now and strangely more at peace within myself. We now have to put our efforts into making Connors' future the best it can be for all our benefits. To ensure he has the best education and care that is available to him. Right now he is very happy just being who he is, but he will become more aware of being different as he gets older. He will need to learn how to cope in a world that struggles to understand him. We will need to be there to support him and help him along the way. We know that he is a sensitive, intelligent and caring little boy, who with the right guidance, can grow to become a kind, responsible, hard working adult.

I hope you have found this book inspiring and helpful. To anyone facing similar circumstances I would say that however bleak things may look, never give up the hope of a better future. I used to see Connor as my life sentence, with no chance of parole. Now I see him as a very challenging, funny, exceptional little boy, and I love him with all my heart. Each day we fight a new battle, overcome another problem. We may never come close to winning the war, but we will keep on fighting.

## THE END

# Epilogue

It is summer, 2012. So there you have it, the last ten years of my life. My heart, soul, and emotions laid bare for all to see. Its taken years to write, a decade to live, and you read it in what – a few days, a week or two, a month tops? I hope you enjoyed the journey, feel that you know us a little, and learned something about the complexities of coping with a condition such as autism.

Tom is now settled at his secondary school, revelling in the freedom that his age and maturity now affords him. Connor will be moving on in September, another school to get to know; a whole new chapter of his life starting. Baby Daniel is already nearly two, and has a bright red T-shirt with the words 'little man, BIG ATTITUDE', it sums him up perfectly. Connor is desperate for him to grow up, to stop nibbling the corners off his drawings, and trashing his bedroom. They fight and argue and cry, but already we can see a brotherly bond forming that will last a lifetime.

So it's time to sign off now and say goodbye. I'd be eternally grateful though if you could do just one thing for me, if you don't mind. When you close the cover, resigning us to a place on a dusty bookshelf, take one last look at his picture on the front. Study that face, that beautiful smile, those deep brown eyes staring back at you in all innocence. Remember that all he craves is to be understood, loved, and accepted. If you ever meet us when you're out and about, stop and say hello. A friendly smile and a wave as you walk on by would mean so much more than you can ever imagine.

THANK YOU

FOR READING

OUR STORY